I Am Perhaps Dying

The Medical Backstory of Spinal Tuberculosis Hidden in the Civil War Diary of LeRoy Wiley Gresham

Praise for

The War Outside My Window: The Civil War Diary of LeRoy Wiley Gresham, 1860 - 1865, edited by Janet E. Croon

"A remarkable diary. . . . kept by a Georgia teenager coping with a fatal disease, it affords modern readers the best record I have encountered of the daily suffering and treatment of a terminally ill person during the Civil War era. . . . Alternately instructive, moving, and disturbing, this diary deserves a wide audience."

— Gary W. Gallagher, Nau Professor of History, University of Virginia

"*The War Outside My Window* is really a window looking into the thoughts and perceptions of a doomed teenager who watched the Confederacy die even as he was dying himself."

— William C. Davis, author of *Inventing Loreta Velasquez*

"There are between twelve and fifteen book awards related to the American Civil War. *The War Outside My Window: The Civil War Diary of LeRoy Wiley Gresham, 1860-1865* will likely be nominated several times as a 'book of the year'."

— Rea Redd, the Civil War Librarian blog

"A powerful, entertaining, and insightful glimpse into the world of the Civil War from an unlikely author. . . . Covering serious topics such as slavery and politics as well as the more light-hearted concerns of a young boy, Gresham's account reminds us that the war touched those far removed from the battlefield even as the more routine aspects of life continued."

— Caroline E. Janney, author of *Remembering the Civil War*

"LeRoy Wiley Gresham's short, painful life in Macon ended about the same time as the Civil War, but he left behind a legacy treasured by historians."

— *Macon Telegraph*

"LeRoy Wiley Gresham was a fascinating young man possessed of wit, insight, and eloquence, all while suffering from the ravages of a terminal disease. His diary is simultaneously fascinating, insightful, compelling, and tragic. . . . It deserves a wide audience well beyond the Civil War community."

— Eric J. Wittenberg, award-winning Civil War historian

"What do I know about diaries? Here's what I can say: You have *never* read anything like this. It will appeal to the armchair historian in you (particularly if you've ever dabbled in being a Civil War buff); It will appeal if you want an idea of what everyday life was like 150 years ago; There's a medical case study, too. This combination of themes is impossible to find anywhere else. This won't be the easiest read you come across this year (whatever year it is that you come across it), but it'll be one of the most compelling."

— The Irresponsible Reader blog

"In a tragic parallel to Gresham's record of the demise of the Southern Confederacy, the invalid unknowingly documents his own painful path toward death."

— *Fredericksburg Free-Lance Star*

"Without the efforts of Croon, Savas, and Rasbach, LeRoy Gresham's voice, which speaks as powerfully to us from the past as does that of Anne Frank, would have continued to be unheard. Readers will remember LeRoy long after the covers of the book have closed. As sad and difficult as this book is to read, it is definitely an important addition to the understanding of the Southern home front."

— Meg Groeling, Emerging Civil War blog

"LeRoy's original diary manuscript, kept in the Library of Congress, has now been published as *The War Outside My Window: The Civil War Diary of LeRoy Wiley Gresham, 1860-1865*. No other published account by an educated civilian male teenager (who was also terminally ill) exists."

— *Parade Magazine*

"LeRoy Gresham's gritty diary demonstrates that bravery was not the sole province of fighting men during the Civil War."

— *Civil War Times* magazine

I Am Perhaps Dying

The Medical Backstory of Spinal Tuberculosis
Hidden in the Civil War Diary of LeRoy Wiley Gresham

Dennis A. Rasbach, MD, FACS

Savas Beatie
California

Library of Congress Cataloging-in-Publication Data

Names: Rasbach, Dennis A., author. | Supplement to (work): Gresham, LeRoy Wiley, 1847-1865. The War Outside My Window.
Title: I Am Perhaps Dying: The Medical Backstory of Spinal Tuberculosis Hidden in the Civil War Diary of LeRoy Wiley Gresham / Dennis A. Rasbach.
Description: First edition. | California: Savas Beatie [2018] | Medical supplement to The War Outside My Window: The Civil War Diary of LeRoy Wiley Gresham, 1860-1865 / Janet Elizabeth Croon, ed. El Dorado Hills,

California: Savas Beatie, [2018]. | Includes bibliographical references and index.
Identifiers: LCCN 2018019244| ISBN 9781611214505 (pbk: alk. paper) | ISBN 9781940669892 (ebk)
Subjects: | MESH: Gresham, LeRoy Wiley, 1847-1865. | Tuberculosis, Spinal—diagnosis | Tuberculosis, Spinal—history | Delivery of Health Care—history | American Civil War | Personal Narratives as Topic | Georgia
Classification: LCC RC310 | NLM WE 11 AG4 | DDC 616.99/5009034—dc23
LC record available at https://lccn.loc.gov/2018019244

First edition, first printing.

SB

Savas Beatie LLC
989 Governor Drive, Suite 102
El Dorado Hills, CA 95762

Phone: 916-941-6896
(web) www.savasbeatie.com
(E-mail) sales@savasbeatie.com

Savas Beatie titles are available at special discounts for bulk purchases in the United States by corporations, institutions, and other organizations. For more details, please contact Savas Beatie, P.O. Box 4527, El Dorado Hills, CA 95762, or you may e-mail us at sales@savasbeatie.com, or visit our website at www.savasbeatie.com for additional information.

Proudly published, printed, and warehoused in the United States of America.

To LeRoy Wiley Gresham,

who unwittingly left posterity one of the most
extraordinary medical accounts of life with tuberculosis in the nineteenth century,

and to

my publisher Theodore P. Savas,

whose heart was deeply touched by LeRoy's story, and who felt
compelled to share it with the world.

Table of Contents

Publisher's Preface

Until the spring of 2017, I had never heard of LeRoy Wiley Gresham. Odds are you hadn't either.[1]

Jan Croon, a former teacher and friend on social media living and working in northern Virginia, passed on a link to me of a 2012 article by Michael E. Ruane in the *Washington Post* entitled "Invalid boy's diary focus of Library of Congress Civil War exhibit." I receive articles like this almost daily, so I nearly skipped past it. What a mistake that would have been. I clicked the link and started reading. The lengthy story mesmerized me from the first few sentences.

The Library of Congress was featuring a large display of Civil War material to mark its sesquicentennial, among them "Gresham's little-known diary"—a seven-volume account donated by the family in the 1980s. The writer was a nearly bedridden teenage boy from a wealthy slave-holding family in Macon, Georgia. Some years earlier he had badly broken a leg that never fully healed. How he had hurt it was a mystery left unaddressed.

LeRoy (or just "Loy" to his family) spent 1860-1865 recording what he read, heard, observed, thought, felt, and experienced. He was a voracious reader and devoured everything he could get his hands on, including Shakespeare and Charles Dickens. Arithmetic and word problems fascinated him, as did railroads, science, and chess—a game he played at every opportunity. Most of his time outside was spent in a small custom-built wagon, pulled around town

---

1 This preface, with minor modification for use in this book, appeared originally in Janet E. Croon, ed., *The War Outside my Window: The Civil War Diary of LeRoy Wiley Gresham, 1860-1865* (Savas Beatie, 2018).

by a slave about his own age or his own older brother Thomas. His last diary entry was June 9, 1865. He died eight days later.

By the time I finished reading the article, my fascination with the young lad had changed to one of curiosity. According to the Library of Congress, this remarkable account had yet to be published. The article was five years old, so surely his diaries were now readily available in book form. I searched the Internet and found a second article, this one written two years later in 2014 by the same reporter in the same paper titled "Mary Gresham's grief over invalid son's death echoes from 1865." The focus of this piece was a seven-page private letter written by LeRoy's mother Mary to her sister shortly after LeRoy died. Mary's tender soaring prose included a detailed description of LeRoy's final hours. Her palpable pain at his passing tugs at one's heart strings and is, even now, difficult to read.

I kept searching. To my astonishment, other than tangential references to LeRoy or the Gresham family, there was not a single word about the diaries having been published, or that anyone was even considering doing so. How could this be? I followed the link to the Library of Congress website and spent a couple hours reading from the diaries. Then and there I made my decision and picked up the phone.

"Jan, are you interested in transcribing and annotating LeRoy's journals for publication?" Her reply was an enthusiastic "Yes!" A staff member at the Library of Congress soon confirmed there were no restrictions on publishing, and that to her knowledge, no one else was preparing to publish the diaries.

Marketing director Sarah Keeney and I charted a rather expeditious course of action. Once we signed a contract with Jan, we distributed a press release announcing that Savas Beatie would be publishing the book the following year—an admittedly aggressive schedule. My hope was that the news would flush out other efforts farther along than our own, and so save us an inordinate amount of time and money. It also might discourage anyone who was thinking of transcribing and publishing them. Because of his obvious interest in LeRoy's remarkable story, I emailed a copy of the press release to *Washington Post* reporter Michael Ruane. Michael quickly replied that he was pleased LeRoy's efforts would be published, and to keep him informed as the work progressed. Michael would almost certainly have known if someone else was working on the diaries.

It looked as if the way ahead was clear.

*   *   *

LeRoy Gresham was 12 years old when he began writing in his first journal in 1860. The blank book was a gift from his mother so he could record his experiences with his father, John Gresham, on their upcoming trip to Philadelphia to see a medical specialist about LeRoy's "condition." Apparently his unhealed crushed leg was getting worse. How had he broken it?

Further research uncovered a newspaper account written many decades after the event by Macon native Albert Martin Ayres in which he reminisced about his time growing up in Georgia. It included a story about an accident that had crushed a young boy's leg and left him a cripple when a chimney collapsed on him and inflicted the painful and crippling injury that left eight-year-old LeRoy a prisoner within his own young body.[2]

LeRoy and his father made the 1,400-mile round trip by sea from Savannah to Philadelphia to seek an effective treatment. Unfortunately, there was nothing the Northern specialist could do for the young man except prescribe some medicine (presumably for pain) and recommend "extended rest." The disappointed father and son returned to Macon, where LeRoy kept writing. Deep in the heart of Georgia, mostly from reclined positions, he put pen to paper with a vim and often tongue-in-cheek vigor that impresses even now, almost 160 years later.

The youngster soaked in everything around him. He read books and devoured newspapers and magazines. He listened to gossip and discussed and debated important social and military topics with his parents, older brother Thomas, other relatives, and family friends. He recorded his thoughts nearly every day.

His early daily logs began with unpretentious observations about the weather and his sea journey and visits to Philadelphia and New York. LeRoy wrote for the next five years about politics and the secession movement, the long and increasingly destructive Civil War, life in Macon at the center of a socially prominent slave-holding family, his interactions with many of the slaves, and his multitude of hobbies and interests. His straightforward and (usually) well-organized journals are riddled with doodles, math and word

---

2   Iris Margaret Ayres Smale, *Albert Martin Ayres I Memoirs* (LuLu, 2004), 8.

problems, charts of chess moves and games, lists of books he read, poetry, religious references, drawings, and even detailed tables recording the weather.

It quickly becomes clear LeRoy's diary became an important part of his life. He wrote about his extended family in Macon, Sparta, and Athens, where his grandmother (who had six living sons who served in the Civil War) resided. LeRoy marveled as Macon, "safe" in a central location in the Deep South, evolved into one of the Confederacy's most important industrial centers. Tens of thousands of Southern troops passed through the important railroad city. Thousands more trained there and left for the front. Union prisoners were confined there. LeRoy witnessed it all.

As the years progressed, so did LeRoy's capacity to reason, analyze, and expound. His ability to handle major events in a concise and crisp manner is surprising for one so young. What began with uncomplicated simple observations evolved into complex and nuanced entries. He learned to take early reports of important military events with a grain of salt, and to question the truth of what he was being told or reading in the papers. Late-war entries reflect disagreements with his father (whom he adored) about the course of the bloody war, and demonstrate his healthy skepticism regarding political pro-nouncements. His pen occasionally dripped vitriol. He found it easy to mock politicians or generals he disliked, and he often did so with gusto. Despite the depressing nature of his world, most of his entries were penned with a certain irrepressible youthful optimism laced with clever hilarity and grin-inducing charm. Clever Twain-like phrases sprinkled throughout capture his precocious nature.

And then there is the matter of slavery. Human bondage is a stain on humanity; it existed at some point or another in every country in the world, and this one fought a long bloody war—the central feature of these journals—that ended it. Slaves were omnipresent in LeRoy's short life. He was born a rich plantation-owner's son, so slavery to him was the only way of life he ever knew. Unfortunately, he did not elaborate at any depth about the institution. Because he was so young and so sick, and was moving toward adulthood as fast as he was to the grave, it is doubtful he had the requisite time to reach any firm conclusions about the morality and ethics of slavery.

It is important to keep in mind that this is a primary source from another time—a time into which LeRoy was born and raised. It should therefore come as no surprise that he used terms freely that are not socially acceptable today. This says little about LeRoy other than that he was a product of his age, upbringing, and social status. He used words like "darkies" or "nigs" or "negroes" descriptively, not pejoratively. He wrote often about the Gresham slaves by name and detailed their comings and goings and changing relationships with the family as the war progressed. Many entries exhibit an obvious affection or concern, as the situation dictated. He was born and raised with slave-servants in the Macon home. Some, like Frank, had carpentry skills and helped LeRoy build things, while Julia Ann and others cooked much of their food, and Bill and Allen pulled him around town in his wagon. It is difficult to imagine that someone like LeRoy, living his entire life in proximity with them, would not form some sort of bond under such circumstances. As he matures, he offers a few clues on this subject; I leave it to readers to reach their own conclusions.

The overriding theme of these diaries is the Civil War, but there is something else lurking within these pages, something dark, menacing, and ultimately, horrific that will eventually become clear to readers: The gifted teenager was suffering from much more than a crushed leg that had not healed properly. He was ill, and his condition slowly, if steadily, worsened until his young body finally gave out. What, exactly, had killed LeRoy at such a young age?

For help with a diagnosis, I reached out to Dennis Rasbach, an experienced general surgeon for whom the Civil War is a serious avocation. Intrigued by the challenge, he rolled up his sleeves and began unraveling the mystery. LeRoy's own writings offered more than enough clues. He recorded his many symptoms, his array of treatments (one might charitably describe as pharmaceutical roulette), and his horrendous suffering—often in agonizing detail. Additional medical and historical research, coupled with discussions with other disease experts, confirmed Dr. Rasbach's suspicions: The Macon teenager had been fighting and losing his battle with a fatal disease for several years. It was this very illness that had prompted his father to take his son north to see Dr. Pancoast as the diary opens. In fact, local doctors had diagnosed his disease in early 1857 in news that crushed his loving parents. LeRoy's ill-healed broken leg had nothing to do with his trip north. Dr. Rasbach contributed both a Medical Foreword, and a more lengthy Medical Afterword, in *The War Outside My Window*.

LeRoy's parents and doctors (and eventually, and almost certainly, his older brother Thomas) knew exactly what he was suffering from, and that he was terminally ill. For reasons that are their own, no one shared the news with

LeRoy, who, unbeknownst to him, was chronicling his own slow and painful descent toward death in tandem with the demise of the Southern Confederacy. Finally, when he was too weak to write, eat, and barely able to speak, he looked up from his deathbed to quietly announce, "Well, Mother, this is the end," to which Mary Gresham asked, "What do you mean, my Son?" His five-word reply broke her heart: "I am dying, ain't I?" LeRoy passed away the next day, just weeks after the Confederacy's final field army surrendered. He was just 17.

In addition to being a publisher, I am a trained historian who has been studying the Civil War for a half-century. To my knowledge, no other male teenage civilian, North or South, left a diary spanning the entire Civil War; certainly one like this has never been published. Most that have found their way into print were penned by soldiers like Confederate Sam Watkins (*Company Aytch: A Sideshow of the Big Show*) and Unionist Elisha Rhodes (*All for the Union: The Civil War Diary and Letters of Elisha Hunt Rhodes*). Others were kept by adults who lived and mingled in high society, like Southern aristocrat Mary Chesnut (*A Diary from Dixie*), wealthy Louisianan Sarah Morgan (*A Confederate Girl's Diary*), and Northern attorney George Templeton Strong (*The Diary of George Templeton Strong*). LeRoy was not a soldier or an adult, and he rarely left home.

When I asked editor Jan Croon whether anything similar to LeRoy's effort came to mind, the former teacher suggested a faint resemblance to *The Diary of Anne Frank*. It is not a perfect comparison, for Anne was persecuted because she was Jewish, and her account is justly venerated as being in a class of its own. Still, there are several parallels worth considering. Both journals were kept by adolescents during wartime, and both were keen observers of societies undergoing radical change. Both were eloquent writers, especially given their age, and each offers readers a detailed record of their daily experiences. There is another similarity, less obvious but deeply influential. Anne and LeRoy both observed their changing worlds at a distance. Anne spent years hiding and writing from the confines of secret rooms to avoid arrest by the Nazis. LeRoy was also confined, though by a physical ailment that kept him nearly immobile, mostly housebound, and largely unable to take part in the society in which he lived. He could not attend school or church, he missed nearly every major local event (including many family affairs), and he could only watch from the rolling confinement of his wagon as his friends played "town ball," an early form of baseball. LeRoy's main threat came not from Nazis, or even from the Union "invaders" who would eventually occupy his home, but from within his own body as it slowly weakened and withered away.

I Am Perhaps Dying explains the medical back story of the internal invasion that ransacked LeRoy Gresham's heath and claimed his life as he was watching, through the window of his confinement, the parallel destruction of the society into which he had been born. It provides essential context for the larger diary by enabling the reader to more fully enter into the atmosphere of the Gresham home, where echoes of coughing around the clock were constant reminders that a beloved son, brother, or young master was wasting away, destined to depart the family circle sooner rather than later.

With a fuller understanding of LeRoy's medical condition in hand, pick up a copy of *The War Outside My Window* and enjoy it with this insight in mind. As you do so, consider that in some ways you are now reading the diary from the perspective of the parents, who knew what was eventually coming even if their beloved son did not. Perhaps you will be as surprised as I was to learn that the mood inside the home on College Street in Macon was not as dark and foreboding as one might expect.

Now, you too have heard of LeRoy Wiley Gresham. I am confident you will think of him and of his terrible disease long after you finish this book.

Theodore P. Savas
Publisher

Author's Preface

As noted in the preceding Publisher's Preface, I contributed a Medical Foreword and a Medical Afterword in *The War Outside My Window*. Why, then, did I also produce a medical supplement to accompany that book?

The answer has partly to do with the multifaceted nature of LeRoy Gresham's writing, which spans the gamut of life events that were of interest to a precocious southern teenager—among them, the military, political, religious, social, literary, meteorological and dietary matters of the day. If the scope of the book were limited to these observations alone, the work would rank as an important contribution to our understanding of life and times in the South during the war years of the mid-nineteenth century.

Sadly, a separate dark thread winds through the diary. Chronic disease and suffering lie close to the surface, stalking the young writer. Gresham's personal struggle heightens the drama of the narrative, showcasing the resilience and courage of a plucky young invalid, and demonstrating to us that such qualities are not limited to fields of armed conflict. Tragically, the destiny of heroes, whether they are to be found in the sick bed or on the battlefield, is often a premature death, and in this instance, that is what finally shatters the window.

For some, the external historical and sociological aspects of this diary are ample grist for contemplation and study. But, if the book tugs at your heart, as it does mine (and *especially* if you are medically oriented), the story of LeRoy's personal struggle against an invisible internal foe eclipses everything else. As the war inside moves to center stage, life outside the window becomes almost a distraction, with the focus shifting to a search for explanations of what is happening to LeRoy himself, and why. It is for readers who find themselves so moved that *I Am Perhaps Dying* is targeted.

The agent responsible for LeRoy Gresham's demise turns out to be Mycobacterium tuberculosis, a tiny but lethal adversary of humanity since the beginning of recorded time. In the second half of the nineteenth century, tuberculosis was the deadliest disease in the world, accounting for one-third of all deaths. Even today, a quarter of the world's population is infected with TB, and the disease remains one of the top ten causes of death, claiming 1.7 million lives annually, mostly in poor and underdeveloped countries.

One reason why medical training is so intensive and time consuming is that physicians must be able to spot occasional zebras among the horses. It's always exciting to find one, whether in clinical practice or in historical diagnosis. Thankfully, what would have been classified as a horse during the Civil War era (and remains so in parts of our world) has become a zebra for many of us today. According to recent CDC statistics, fewer than 10,000 new cases of TB were reported in the USA in 2016, and fewer than 500 people died from it; more than two-thirds of all new cases occurred in individuals who were born outside of this country. Thus, tuberculosis has become a medical rarity here in the United States. We certainly have been blessed by modern scientific progress!

As a physician with more than forty years of experience in medicine, I can recall having seen only one or two cases of active TB when I was a student in East Baltimore in the 1970s. I have never observed a patient with a hunchback or gibbus deformity. I have never known a patient to die of tuberculosis. I feel very confident in saying that my personal inexperience with the disease mirrors that of the majority of physicians throughout North America today.

Modern-day unfamiliarity with TB in the developed world is a mixed blessing. It goes hand-in-hand with a certain complacency toward the disease as a threat to life and happiness as a result of our confidence that it can usually be cured with a course of drug therapy. This was not the case in the mid-nineteenth century, when a diagnosis of tuberculosis was akin to having Ebola or a lethal form of cancer today. Treatments were largely ineffective and unpleasant. The medical world was on the cusp of major discoveries in microbiology, anesthesia, radiology, surgery, and pharmacology, but those disciplines were in nascent stages of development. None had advanced to be of much help in the understanding of, or in the treatment of tuberculosis at the time.

One hundred and fifty years later, medical professionals and the lay public alike have lost all sense of context for evaluating and comprehending concepts such as "issues" made by caustics and maintained by peas, or of hypophosphites, rest therapy, and other modalities that were commonly employed in earlier times to treat tuberculosis. While we may be tempted to look back dismissively on the "primitive" and ultimately ineffective methods that our forebears devised to combat the major pestilence of their century— what a PBS documentary has recently labeled The Forgotten Plague[1]—we should never lose sight of the fact that the people who lived before us were every bit as intelligent as we imagine ourselves to be, were often much more observant, and were possessed of keen powers of deductive reasoning. Many physicians and scientists of the nineteenth century, in fact, became the pioneers upon whose shoulders the foundations of modern medicine firmly rest.

A note about the title: "I am perhaps . . ." is the last entry in the diary of LeRoy Wiley Gresham. It was written on June 9, 1865, by his mother Mary, just nine days before LeRoy took his last breath. Up to that point, there is no indication that the young man had any awareness his life was ebbing away, or that he had an appointment with an early death. Although Gresham's doctors and his parents knew—perhaps as early as the winter of 1857—that the nine-year-old boy was afflicted with the usually fatal disease we now know as tuberculosis, there is no evidence any of them shared the diagnosis with the boy, and in fact, the evidence contained in a letter written by his mother to her sister shortly after his death confirms he did not know he was fatally ill until the day before he died.

With the benefit of omniscient hindsight, we, too, now know what lies ahead, making it all the more heart-rending as we watch LeRoy, standing alone in the dark, experiencing deferred hope and unfulfilled expectations, and yet courageously grasping life by the horns.

I Am Perhaps Dying is a journey that I was compelled to make for myself. I offer it to others who, like me, might find themselves intrigued by the physical ordeal of an unfortunate, but very brave and likeable young man from a past era. To those who are drawn to peer deeper inside the window that he has opened, I invite you to enter somberly and to sift with me through these riddled remains, as together we search for insights and understanding.

Dennis A. Rasbach, MD, FACS

---

1   http://www.pbs.org/wgbh/americanexperience/films/plague/.

Introduction

When the Library of Congress first displayed excerpts from the seven-volume 1860-1865 diary of LeRoy Wiley Gresham in 2012, it was done as part of a Civil War exhibit. In addition to remarks about daily civic, religious and family life in a small, relatively rural Georgia community, they have much to say about the politics and the conduct of the Civil War. Thus, it comes as no surprise that when a leading publisher of military history decided to transcribe and release the diary in print, the emphasis would be on the external conflict that was defining the times—*The War Outside My Window*. But windows are two-way portals, and outside observers can also peer within the glass. In this particular diary, the drama unfolding in the experience of a single individual turns out to be every bit as compelling as the story of the devastation that was being inflicted on the southern people in the wake of their secession from the Union.

Publisher Theodore Savas quickly recognized the importance of the intimate, personal aspect of the journals and the charisma of the adolescent author, who winsomely draws the reader into the world of current events, hobbies, food and family traditions, novels, poetry, mathematical and word problems, chess moves, transportation, and meteorological phenomena of his times. Tragically, the young diarist is an invalid, and both he and the Confederacy to which has pledged his allegiance are unwittingly hurtling down parallel paths to an unhappy ending. As the spring of 1865 rolls around, the writer seems mercifully unaware that neither he nor the secession movement will survive the coming of another summer.

It is only natural to speculate on the cause of the premature death of the amiable and courageous young author, who met his Maker at the tender age of seventeen. Most observers have attributed his demise to complications from an injury he received on September 21, 1856, when a brick chimney collapsed, crushing his left leg. A series of setbacks followed in the wake of that accident. But the question begs to be answered: could a fractured leg fully explain the depth and scope of suffering that befell young LeRoy Gresham over the next nine years?

In search of an answer, Ted Savas asked me to carefully review the diary from the perspective of a twenty-first century surgeon. Eager to undertake the task, I soon found myself engrossed in the work of a medical detective, sifting through details in the historical documents. As had been my prior experience in researching battlefield accounts at Petersburg, the assignment proved immensely rewarding and full of unexpected discoveries, and the answer to the fundamental question came as a total surprise. The analysis led to the unmistakable conclusion that LeRoy Wiley Gresham suffered from advanced pulmonary and spinal tuberculosis (Pott's disease). He almost certainly had Pott's disease when he made a journey to consult with a specialist in Philadelphia in 1860, at the beginning of his journal, and he may have had signs of TB as early as 1857, seven months after the accident that crushed his leg. In the terminal stages of his life, he was showing signs of oropharyngeal and gastrointestinal tuberculosis, as well as of symptoms of clinical depression, the emergence of which coincided with the unfavorable conclusion of the war.

Today we understand tuberculosis as an infectious disease, caused by a mycobacterium. Specific and effective treatments are available, although a battle is constantly being waged against resistant strains. In LeRoy Gresham's day, however, there was no understanding of a "germ theory" of disease, and no specific treatments existed. Almost everyone who developed active tuberculosis died of it, sooner or later.

Also known as "consumption," "phthisis" (via Latin, from Greek, meaning "wasting away"), and the "white plague," tuberculosis was a prolific killer in the nineteenth century, claiming more lives than any other disease. Many of its victims came from among the young working poor of urban centers. However, no demographic was spared, and the prevalence of the illness among artists, writers and musicians led to a peculiar positive association of tuberculosis with the romantic spirit of the era. Composer Frederic Chopin died of tuberculosis.

John Keats, Edgar Allan Poe, Charlotte Brontë, and Fyodor Dostoevsky wrote about it in their poems and novels, and the disease was depicted operatically in Verdi's La traviata and Puccini's La bohème.

Despite the popularity of TB as a literary motif, there is a paucity of extended accounts charting an individual's personal experience with the malady as it evolved over time, before effective treatments became available. Thus, Gresham's diary is a rare chronicle of consumption, providing a window into an affliction that must have been very prevalent among families on both sides of the conflict that was rending our nation at the time.

The War outside My Window, the Civil War Diary of LeRoy Wiley Gresham, 1860-1865 contains elements that are certain to attract the attention of students from a variety of disciplines. Civil War historians, sociologists, specialists in education and child development, genealogists, and many others will find their own particular streams of interest to explore. However, the medical significance of the journals is nothing short of extraordinary.

The aim of this short work is to provide a focus on those medical aspects of the diary. Our hope is that this supplement will have a special appeal for laymen, practitioners, and scholars with particular interest in the diseases and medical practices of the nineteenth century, and that it will provide a roadmap for the use of the valuable primary source in subsequent investigations within the various disciplines of medicine and medical history.

Acknowledgments:

I wish to express my profound appreciation to Janet Croon for her tireless work in transcribing and abstracting pertinent medical comments from the diary of LeRoy Wiley Gresham; to Ted Savas and all the wonderful people at Savas Beatie, for their consistently excellent editorial and publishing support; and to my wonderful wife Ellen, for her loving presence, helpful comments, and encouraging words throughout the researching and writing of I Am Perhaps Dying. I believe that each of us can honestly say that we have grown to love the courageous young man whose story we have unfolded together.

The process has been thoroughly enriching for me personally, and I am most grateful to have shared the journey with these fellow-travelers.

DAR

1

Historical Diagnosis I

Clues from Symptoms

In medicine, a symptom is something a person notices as a departure from his normal state of feeling or function— for instance, pain or nausea. Symptoms are subjective. A sign is objective evidence of disease that is observable by others—temperature elevation, jaundice and palpable tumors are examples. Gresham's journals deal exclusively with the symptoms and signs of his infirmity.

Diagnosis is the process of gathering and analyzing information to identify the underlying nature or cause of an illness. Whereas treatments can be prescribed on the basis of symptoms alone (an analgesic to mask or control pain, for instance), diagnosing the root cause of an illness provides a firmer foundation for precise and effective treatment. This is especially important when multiple symptoms coexist. Knowing the etiology of a disorder is fundamental to finding its cure.

Practitioners of earlier eras categorized diseases almost exclusively on the basis of symptoms and physical findings. They had no scanning instruments with which to peer inside the body, and laboratory methods for detecting abnormal pathology or altered physiology at a cellular or molecular level were very rudimentary.

In reading the medical portions of LeRoy's diary, we may initially feel handicapped by the absence of a unifying diagnostic "label" for his condition. His doctors, as we shall see, almost certainly had one, but they either did not reveal it to him, or he chose not to share it with the readers of his journals. Fortunately, there are enough clues in the writing to allow us to piece together

LeRoy Wiley Gresham circa 1860. *Library of Congress*

an accurate twenty-first century diagnosis, after engaging in a bit of medical detective work.

Obtaining an account of past medical events is always an important part of the diagnostic process. In this case, the pertinent element is the history of a major traumatic injury in childhood. LeRoy was eight years old when the bricks of a chimney collapsed on him, crushing his left leg. It seemed that this accident had been at the root of his troubles, but it is important not to jump to hasty conclusions. The progression of symptoms seems to far surpass the suffering that one would normally expect from a broken leg. A good diagnostician will reserve the possibility that the accident might have been merely a coincidence— a red herring in the chain of events that led to the patient's demise, or perhaps a contributing, but not necessarily a primary causal factor.

As the diary opens, the lad is twelve and a half years old, and he is about to embark with his father on a voyage of more than 800 miles by sea to Philadelphia for the purpose of consulting with a specialist, presumably concerning his broken leg and accompanying back pain. Surprisingly, Doctor Joseph Pancoast pronounces his condition better than expected, and prescribes only some medicine, along with "issues and lying down for the summer."

What follows confounds our expectations of the course of a boy with a gimpy leg. It is not surprising there would be pain, but LeRoy's complaints are centered more in his back than in his injured leg. Belladonna plasters and Jimson weed salves are prescribed, along with opium-derived drugs to quell the discomfort. A wagon is constructed to provide some mobility, and to enable the invalid to avoid becoming completely bed-ridden. However, the lad's troubles only multiply and intensify.

Despite the fact the original injury was to his leg, LeRoy's most vexing symptom turns out to be a chronic cough. He refers to it more than any other symptom—over 200 times. First mentioned in February, 1861, it quickly becomes "incessant," "troublesome," "obstreperous," "exhausting," "annoying beyond measure," "a continual hacking." It persists as a central feature throughout the narrative. The cough is especially bothersome at night—as soon as he lies down, sometimes all through the night. Later on, it becomes diurnal and productive of phlegm. Headache and insomnia often accompany the coughing. The writer refers to his disturbed sleep more than 130 times during the five-year span of his writing.

Fevers then begin to punctuate the narrative, at first intermittently; then, in early 1863, occurring frequently in the evenings, along with night sweats.

The young man becomes consumed by a general wasting and debility. In November, 1863, he weighs only 63 pounds, which is well below the CDC's 5th percentile (105 pounds) and less than half of the weight at the 50th percentile (135 pounds) for a sixteen-year-old boy today.

LeRoy develops an open sore on his back. We could postulate that it might have been a pressure sore—a decubitus ulcer from his confinement to bed and wagon. But could it have been something more? Plasters and salves and liniments are employed to treat the back pain and sores, but the young patient goes on to develop abscesses, first on the left side of his back, and later on both sides. His father paints them with iodine. Dr. Fitzgerald drains them. In 1863, they are "running freely," discharging large quantities of pus continually, which suggests a large, deep and incompletely evacuated source of infection.

As the pain intensifies, LeRoy's back becomes weaker, so that he cannot sit up without pain. By February, 1863, his grandmother has devised a corset-like garment for his torso that laces up, giving him support for his spine, and improved comfort. Nevertheless, his hips ache all night long, and he develops new pain in his breast and shoulder.

On May 23, 1864, he writes, "One joint of my spine, right between the abscesses is very sore and you can see the matter, as it runs from the joint to the abscess."

In early 1865, the throat is sore and swollen. Dyspepsia, anorexia, nausea, vomiting, cholera-like diarrhea, and finally bloody dysentery follow.

By May, the previously uninjured right leg is now being drawn up with contractures, as the left one was earlier.

Eventually the pain-wracked, emaciated and exhausted body of LeRoy Wiley Gresham can endure no more. The courageous young man succumbs on June 18, 1865, at the age of seventeen.

What was the ultimate cause of this untimely death? Was it the fallen chimney that broke the boy's leg more than eight years earlier? Given the progressive advance of dysfunction in multiple organ systems—pulmonary, musculoskeletal, integumentary, nervous, and gastrointestinal—and the systemic wasting and fevers, that explanation seems extremely unlikely.

The most plausible unifying diagnosis, based on the constellation of symptoms recorded in the journals, is that LeRoy Wiley Gresham suffered from the scourge of tuberculosis. In arriving at this conclusion, statistical probability is solidly on our side, as TB was the leading cause of death from disease in the latter half of the nineteenth century, and it was the killer of nearly half of the young Americans who died between the ages of 15 and 35.

Also known as "phthisis" and "consumption," tuberculosis was characterized by fatigue, night sweats, and a general "wasting away" of the victim, along with the persistent coughing-up of thick white phlegm. LeRoy's chronic cough and classic constitutional symptoms of fever, night sweats and weight loss fit the picture well.

The progression of the disease in this particular case, however, implies more than just pulmonary manifestations of TB. The chronic back pain, weakness, and the development of chronically-draining abscesses on his back, suggest that Gresham was likely a victim of Pott's disease—extra-pulmonary tuberculosis of the spine, extending into the paraspinal muscles and causing the chronic drainage there. As LeRoy so perceptively noted, "as long as there is any disease there [in what he terms a "joint of the spine," i.e., the space between the spinous processes of adjacent vertebrae], the sores cannot heal."

> The natural course of skeletal tuberculosis without chemotherapy passed through three stages spanning 3–5 years. In the "stage of onset", lasting from 1 month to 1 year, the localized disease developed into a warm tender swelling with marked localized osteoporosis and minimal destruction. In the "stage of destruction", lasting 1–3 years, the disease progressed until there was gross destruction of the vertebrae with deformity, subluxation, contractures, and abscess formation. The abscesses finally ruptured and drained as ulcers and sinuses developed frequent secondary pyogenic infection. With superimposed pyogenic infection, the general defense mechanism of the patient became markedly lowered, with severe cachexia, frequent tuberculous dissemination (miliary tuberculosis, tuberculous meningitis), and death in nearly 1/3 of the patients (it is easy to understand why early writers used the term 'consumption').[1]

> Extension of tuberculosis from vertebral and discal sites to the ligaments and soft tissues is frequent. Paravertebral abscesses occur at all levels and may be on one side only, on both sides symmetrically or asymmetrically, or may occur only in front of the spine. The paravertebral abscess may remain localised or extend for a considerable distance.[2]

Not only the drainage, but also the drawing up of his legs can be explained by spinal tuberculosis, which causes a sharp angulation or "gibbus" (hunchback) deformity of the spine, with impingement on the nervous tissue of the spinal cord, potentially leading to paralysis. LeRoy described, near the end of his account, contractures of his good right leg, as well as of the previously injured left one.

---

1   https://www.ncbi.nlm.nih.gov/pmc/articles/PMC3691412/, *Eur. Spine J* 2013 June 22 (Suppl. 4): 529-538. PMCID: PMC3691412.

2   https://pdfs.semanticscholar.org/0645/29ac5aa41376c2a738b3fa4e4ecb90f6ce5e.pdf.

The sore throat and terminal gastrointestinal manifestations of bloody diarrhea are also likely tubercular in origin. Ulcers in the mouth, larynx or gastrointestinal tract were the result of chronic expectoration and swallowing of the patient's own highly infectious pulmonary secretions.

2

Historical Diagnosis II

Clues from Medicines

Historical diagnosticians have the luxury of working backwards, using prescribed remedies to infer a diagnosis. The prescribing pattern of LeRoy's attending physicians is very revealing. Several of the medicines were widely used in the treatment of symptoms of consumption. One was even being promoted as a "specific remedy."

Syrup of the Hypophosphite of Soda, Lime and Potassa— Dr. J. F. Churchill's "Specific Remedy" for Consumption

Thursday January 22nd 1863: . . . Commenced to take my new medicine "The Syrup of the Hypophosphite of Soda, Lime + Potassa." and it is nasty and stinks. It has name enough to cure anything.

An actual bottle from which Dr. J. F. Churchill's "Specific Remedy" was dispensed. *Author*

In December, 1862, LeRoy was taking hyperphosphites, and had been doing so for some time. On January 22, 1863, Dr. White prescribed a new medicine, "Syrup of the Hypophosphite of Soda, Lime + Potassa."

The Compound Syrup of the Hypophosphites, also known as Dr. Churchill's Specific Remedy for Consumption, was the newest medical fad for the treatment of tuberculosis in the 1860's. The syrup was composed of the hypophosphites of iron, lime (calcium), soda (sodium) and potassa (potassium), and was touted as a practical cure for consumption.[1]

The early history of Churchill's remedy has been summarized as follows:

In July 1847, Dr. J. Francis Churchill of Paris and later England, read a paper to the French Academy of Medicine on Tuberculosis. He was putting together his theory on the cause for consumption, by now being called tuberculosis. In 1855, Dr. Churchill coined the "Tubercular Diathesis Theory of Tuberculosis;" a year later he published this theory in Paris as *De la cause immediate et du traitement specifique de la phthisie pulmonaire et des maladies tuberculeuses*. In this writing, Churchill blamed Tuberculosis (or Phthisis as it soon-after came to be known) on poor oxidation. He felt Phosphorous could work to stimulate oxidation in the lung and be turned into a "phosphatide element." He therefore suggested the use of the hypophosphate as a tonic to improve the functionability [sic] of the lung in these people.

Over the next two years, knowledge of this new theory for Tuberculosis reached North America. In 1860, it was introduced to the Physio-Medical profession by the reprinting of Dr. Richard Quinn's London Lancet article on the same subject. This then was published by Cincinnati Medical & Surgical News, a new name for an old journal linked to the most popular form of alternative medicine in the Midwest – Physiomedicine.[2]

The medical community did not unanimously endorse Churchill's views. In 1860, the treatment was already being questioned in the Journal of Rational Medicine:

---

1   Felter, H.W., ed., "New Remedies," *The Eclectic Medical Journal*, Vol. 76, (January to December, 1916), 512-513.

2   Altonen, B. "Dr. Churchill's Cure for Consumption, History and Controversy," in https://brianaltonenmph.com/6-history-of-medicine-and-pharmacy/pacific-northwest-med icine-ca-1820-ca-present/john-kennedy-bristow-1814-1883/research-papers/drchurch hills-cure-for-consumption-history-and-controversy/.

Three years since Dr. J. F. Churchill read a communication to the French Academy of Medicine, laudatory of the Hypophosphites of Lime and Soda in consumption; and since then I have been anxiously looking for any positive and reliable practical results of this treatment. Shortly after Dr. Churchill's paper was read the hypophosphites were tried in the Brompton Hospital for consumption, and failed to prove useful. Again Dr. Churchill published his memoir with Additions; and again his remedies were tried at the Brompton Hospital; and Dr. Quain has published the results obtained, after giving them a full and fair trial. He said: "A review of the preceding facts led me to form a most unfavorable opinion of the value of the hypophosphites in the treatment of phthisis. I believe them to be comparatively, if not absolutely, useless.[3]

In 1861, American physician Dr. James Bennett echoed allegations of a shortage of theoretical justification for, and an absence of proven therapeutic benefit from the administration of hypophosphites to patients with phthisis:

The confidence which Dr. Churchill claims for these salts is founded upon his theory, that tubercular diseases have their origin in a diminution of the oxidizable phosphorus contained in the body, the deficiency of which he attempts to supply by the administration of the hypophosphites of lime and soda, which he says he has found by experiment to be the best adapted for insuring the absorption and assimilation of the deficient element, while the hyperphosphite of lime, by supplying another element assumed to be deficient in the tubercular constitution, he thinks specially adapted to certain cases. Neither the theory nor practice is confirmed by other pathologists and therapeutists.[4]

Disputes within the medical community notwithstanding, hypophosphites continued to be prescribed in many quarters into the beginning of the twentieth century, and the fact remains that in 1862, LeRoy Gresham was being treated with a cutting-edge remedy that was thought by many to be a "silver bullet" for consumption. It is unfortunate that he had to suffer the nasty taste and stink (as noted in his diary) of a concoction that ultimately proved to be completely ineffective against mycobacterial infection.

3   Cleaveland, C.H., ed., "Churchill's Hypophosphites in Phthisis," in *Journal of Rational Medicine*, Vol. I, No. 7 (July, 1860), 220.

4   Bennett, D, "Hypophosphites in the Treatment of Phthisis," in *Pacific Medical and Surgical Journal*, Vol.4 (1861), Selections, 14.

Rockbridge Alum Water

March 27 Wednesday [1861]: . . . Father brought up a bottle of Rockbridge alum water. Not very nice.

Sunday May 19 1861: . . . Father brought me a book Analysis of Rock Bridge Alum Water. If it does all the book says it must be a great thing.

Like the Syrup of the Hypophosphites, Alum water, which LeRoy took in March 1861, tasted very bad. The Medical Association of Virginia would later endorse it by unanimous action and after "thorough examination," for the treatment of patients with scrofula (tuberculous infection of the lymph nodes of the neck) and incipient consumption, among other maladies.[5]

Creosote

Tuesday June 6th 1865 . . . Dr. Hall has prescribed a preparation of Creosote for me to take which he says is one of the best remedies known to the profession.

Creosote was prescribed to control the coughing of pulmonary tuberculosis:

Many cases in the incipient and moderately advanced stages of the disease are immensely relieved by creosote and its derivatives. The method of administration is given elsewhere. In those in whom internal administration does not relieve the cough, we may try the effects of inhalation of creosote, menthol, eucalyptol, tincture of benzoin, etc.[6]

By 1900, creosote was so widely used to treat tuberculosis that it became necessary to emphasize that it was not a specific cure for the disease:

The drug, creosote, has become so inseparably connected in history, in clinical experience, and in present day teachings, with the disease of pulmonary tuberculosis, that its acceptance as a specific becomes a natural consequence. Such empiricism,

---

5   http://exhibits.hsl.virginia.edu/springs/introessay.

6   Fishberg, M, *Pulmonary Tuberculosis* (Lea & Febiger, 1919), 646.

however, is fatal to the scientific treatment of tuberculosis even though creosote does seem to be indicated in every case. Creosote probably exercises its curative action in the lung because of its physiologic property of stimulating the bronchial mucosa, where it is eliminated, and its action as an expectorant; not as a specific for the disease of tuberculosis.[7]

Iodide of Iron

Thursday March 26th 1863: . . . I am taking Iodide of Iron pills. . . .

Saturday July 4th 1863: Father brought me some pills: "Dr. Blanchard's Iodide of Iron." I commenced to take them.

In 1858, the *American Journal of Medical Sciences*, in its "Quarterly Summary of the Improvements and Discoveries in the Medical Sciences," presented a discussion of the value of the iodide of iron in the treatment of tuberculosis. The information was gleaned from a paper that had been printed in a Parisian medical journal in May of that year.

The article cites several French physicians who had employed a syrup of the iodide of iron successfully in the treatment of pulmonary tubercles, and others who had successfully cured advanced abscesses by combining an ingested preparation of the substance with injections of it into the sac of the abscess.

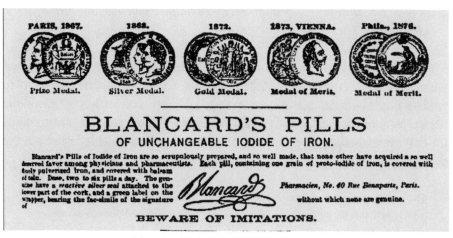

Ad for Blanchard's Pills. *Archives of Ophthalmology*

7   *Journal of the American Medical Association*, 1898; vol. xxxi (18), 1062.

In phthisis, the iodide of iron has been found to act very beneficially, and its importance in this disease will be increased when it is preserved chemically pure, and given in suitable doses . . .. "Recent observations . . . have assigned to iodide of iron an important place among therapeutic agents, and it may be boldly placed among the best medicines which we possess.[8]

Alcohol

August 28 [1861] Wednesday: . . . Mother brought me a large pear and a bottle of extra fine brandy from Mrs. Cobb.

Monday March 24, 1862: . . . took some brandy in going to bed, but did not go to sleep, and had to take a Dover's Powder.

Saturday February 7th 1863: . . . Every night nearly I have a sweat. Father got me a bottle of brandy to take for it.

Sunday February 15th 1863: Cool and pleasant. . . . I would have slept very well but for the heavy + exhausting night sweat which took away my comfort. . . . Took brandy. . . . . I take brandy 3 times per diem.

Sunday, May 14th, 1865: Slept so badly and felt so weak + sick I did not get up. Dr. Hall prescribed for me and sent me some elegant brandy to take every 4 hrs.

Young LeRoy Gresham consumed regular portions of brandy, porter, whiskey and Catawba wine throughout his recorded experience. Modern readers might wonder about such a large quantity and variety of alcoholic beverages appearing in the diary of an "under-aged" teenager. Societal norms of the day aside, this practice becomes much more understandable in light of the then-current theory that alcohol specifically antagonized tuberculosis.

Before the true nature of tuberculosis became apparent, the opinion was somewhat widely held that the subjects of alcoholic excess seldom suffered from consumption or other forms of tuberculosis, and some went so far as to claim that the alcoholic state was

---

8 "Value of Iodide of Iron," in *American Journal of Medical Sciences*, vol LXXII (October, 1858), 516-517.

antagonistic to tuberculosis . . . The idea that alcoholism was in some cases a preventive of tuberculosis may, perhaps, in part account for the advocacy of its persistent and even excessive use in phthisis . . . Bennett also, writing some thirty years since, said: "Of late years, in America, alcohol, especially whiskey, has been much lauded as a remedy in consumption;" but added," I have seen a certain number of cases in which it had been long taken, but I cannot say with benefit . . . Charteris, writing in 1877 concerning the administration of whiskey to phthisical patients, says, "In private practice I order it to be taken ad libitum.[9]

Dr. Austin Flint . . . sings its [alcohol's] praise in season and out of season; and from reading some of his elaborate articles on phthisis, especially his book-reviews in the American Journal of the Medical Sciences, one would conclude that alcohol was the only medicine for the disease. Here is one of his emphatic utterances: "If there be any article in the materia medica which may be considered as in any measure specially efficacious, that is exerting a remedial effect on the morbid condition or cachexia on which the deposit of tubercle depends, we believe it to be alcohol.[10]

Besides being potentially (if not actually) antagonistic to tuberculosis, alcohol was a source of calories to combat cachexia, and also acted as a sedative.

Quinine

Saturday May 17th 1862: . . . Coughed all night. Did not get up to breakfast. Father bought me some quinine pills to stop the fever I have every eve.

Quinine was used to control fever (traditionally in malaria), but also to combat diarrhea, and to facilitate expectoration in tuberculosis:

I have found the hypophosphite of quinine useful in the incipient diarrhoea of phthisis, in that of young children, and occasionally to modify the nature of the expectoration. It has, however, less activity than the other hypophosphites, which is easily accounted for

9 *Transactions of the British Congress on Tuberculosis for the Prevention of Consumption* (London, July 22-26, 1901), 336.

10 Dutcher, A. P., *Pulmonary Tuberculosis: Its Pathology, Nature, Symptoms, Diagnosis, Prognosis, Causes, Hygiene, and Medical Treatment* (J. B. Lippincott & Co., Philadelphia, 1875), 360.

by the small proportion of acid it contains. It is thus useful when the other salts may be found too active.[11]

Dover's Powder

Dover's Powder, a combination of opium and ipecac, was one of LeRoy's primary remedies. He mentions it at least forty-two times in the journal. He typically took it at bedtime, often for treatment of pain and insomnia; but it was also specifically recommended to suppress nocturnal coughing in tuberculosis:

In many cases nothing but opiates gives relief. But in incipient cases opium and its derivatives are to be avoided because it may have to be continued for long periods and, in hopeful cases, the danger of habit formation is not negligible. . . . A dose of Dover's powder may be given in the evening now and then with a view of controlling the cough during the night, but to continue the administration of opium in any form for any length of time is dangerous.[12]

In addition, Dover's powder was used for the treatment of diarrhea associated with gastrointestinal manifestations of tuberculosis:

We have seen that diarrhea in tuberculous is not always due to ulcerations in the intestines and that the latter may exist while the patient

Dover's Powder, one of the popular remedies of the day, containing opium and ipecac. *Author*

11 Churchill, J.F., *Consumption and Tuberculosis: Their Proximate Cause and Specific Treatment by the Hypophosphites* (London, 1875), 67

12 Fishberg, *Pulmonary Tuberculosis*, 664, 646.

is constipated. In many cases the diarrhea is due to chronic catarrh of the bowels induced by swallowed sputum and the patient is to be warned against this very bad habit . . . In many cases medicinal treatment must be given to control the frequent stools . . . Bismuth should be given in doses of 10 to 15 grains five or six times a day. But in most cases opium must be used, more or less. Bismuth . . . may be given in powders combined with fairly large doses of Dover's powder, or the official tincture of opium in 5- to 10-minim doses three or four times a day.[13]

Mustard Plaster

Friday October 18 [1861]: Damp, misty, disagreeable day. . .. I did not sleep well at all. I had a very bad pain in my back and Mother put a mustard plaster on me over which I made a tremendous fuss.

During the nineteenth century, mustard plaster was recommended in the treatment of the chest pain of tuberculosis:

Most of the pains in the chest complained of by tuberculous patients may be relieved by the administration of some placebo, or the application of a mustard plaster, dry cupping, tincture of iodine, etc. In some cases, it is necessary to administer some of the coal-tar analgesics or salicylates. . . . When due to intercurrent pleurisy, strapping of the chest with adhesive plaster is indicated. The pains in the shoulder, often due to diaphragmatic pleurisy, which are very acutely felt especially during the night, are very difficult to manage. The coal-tar analgesics and the salicylates usually give no relief, and often even safe doses of morphine fail. Hot applications to the affected part, or, rarely, the actual cautery, may be necessary.[14]

In reviewing the array of medicines mentioned in the journals, it is impossible to escape the conclusion that they very definitely conform to the pattern of standard treatments being prescribed for the treatment of consumption in the United States and in Europe during the 1860s.

13 Fishberg, *Pulmonary Tuberculosis*, 664.

14 Fishberg, *Pulmonary Tuberculosis*, 661.

3

Historical Diagnosis III

Clues from Physical Treatments

Rest Cure

Sunday, June 24 [1860]: . . . Dr. Pancoast came late at night and prescribed . . . lying down for the summer alas all the year.

Sunday, May 4th 1862: Beautiful bright day. . . . It is 5 years ago since I first lay down. It will soon be two since I laid down this time, and I often wonder whether I am going to get well again.

One of the treatments prescribed by Dr. Joseph Pancoast in June, 1860, was for his young patient to lie down for the summer. This would seem to be a peculiar instruction for someone presenting with a chronic leg deformity nearly four years after a fracture.

In this context, it is interesting to consider the following diary entry from May 4, 1862: "It is 5 years ago today since I first lay down. It will soon be two since I laid down this time."

Nearly two years before the date of this spring, 1862 entry takes us back to the time of the examination by Dr. Pancoast, when rest was prescribed. LeRoy had been mobile enough to make a trip of some 800 miles each way to Philadelphia and New York by boat. He did not have a wagon at the time, and yet he visited the Academy of Natural Science, went to the mint (lying down only because of the extreme heat), went to Sunday services at church, and went out to dinner in Savannah on the way home.

Counting back five years from the day of the anniversary entry takes us to May 4, 1857, seven and a half months after the injury that crushed LeRoy's leg. Normally, confinement might be expected beginning from the time of the initial injury, in the case of a severe fracture, but why should it start seven months later?

J. F. Churchill recited the medical dogma of the times in his 1875 textbook, *Consumption and Tuberculosis*, emphasizing the importance placed on rest in the treatment of patients with TB:

> The first and paramount requirement of diseased lungs as of all other suffering organs is rest. Any amount of exercise which calls from them for any more action than is absolutely necessary to keep up the general health is positively and directly injurious.[1]

Maurice Fishberg, Attending Physician at Montefiore Hospital and Home for Chronic Diseases in New York, provided the following rationale for the role of rest in the treatment of both pulmonary and skeletal forms of tuberculosis, sixty years after it was prescribed for LeRoy:

> We know that Nature makes a strong effort at repairing the affected lung in tuberculosis, but we only rarely think of the method it pursues when doing it. Examining the chest of a tuberculous patient, we find on inspection that there is a strong tendency to putting the affected area of the lung at rest. As already has been shown, during the early stage the muscles overlying the pulmonary lesion are almost invariably rigidly and spasmodically contracted. . . It inhibits or prevents the motion of the underlying lung to a certain extent. Later, pleural adhesions are formed which impede the respiratory movements of the lung to a yet greater extent, as is seen in the lagging of the affected side of the chest, offering favorable conditions for cicatrization. This immobilization of the affected part of the lung also slows the circulation of blood and lymph in that area retains the bacteria and their toxic products, thus lessening toxemia and preventing metastatic auto-infection of unaffected parts of the lung. Rubel has shown experimentally that functional rest greatly contributes toward a cure of tuberculous lesions in the lung.

> Surgeons have utilized physiological and functional rest in the treatment of tuberculosis of bones and joints. The modern treatment of Pott's disease and

---

1 Churchill, *Consumption and Tuberculosis*, 150.

tuberculosis of the various joints consists mainly in affording rest to the affected parts. The splint has done better than the knife in these forms of tuberculosis.[2]

That rest cure was prescribed in 1857 may indicate that LeRoy was suffering from pulmonary tuberculosis at the time, perhaps activated by immunosuppression resulting from the stress and/or bacterial infection attending his leg fracture some months earlier. A letter from LeRoy's father to the boy's mother upon his return from a trip to the family plantation in Houston on January 10, 1857, intimates as much:

> . . . poor Loy seemed happy + cheerful but was not disposed to take much exercise and remained mostly about the house and yard. He stood the ride home very well today + sang + laughed nearly all the way, while my heart was aching with pain. I could think of little else and would often ride with my arms around him – pressing him to me – how little he or any but you knew what I felt. When I lost my hurt boy in your absence – and such a boy – and how to break the news to you myself, I thought the trial severe, but this – who can tell the anguish – I can't write about it + yet I can write about nothing else. Perhaps I was wrong to say I was perfectly miserable. I have yet other blessings left for which I would not be ungrateful. But my poor boy!!

> It was pretty hard work to keep warm last night, and the wind blew as it only blows on this hill + in our room. Thomas slept with me + LeRoy on Minnie's couch. He was heard from all night till was late before we had the courage to reach our toilette this morning. . ..

> PS I shall let Loy go to school in the morning but the Doctors wish to examine him again before giving their advice. I think I should take him North before long . . .

From these few lines, we get the impression that the unfortunate boy has been ambulatory, but lacking in initiative or energy to venture far outside the yard. The father's profound grief, anguish and foreboding seem out of proportion to what one would expect from the parent of a boy who is four months into his recovery from a broken leg, and who is otherwise happy, cheerful, singing and laughing. Something more ominous must underlie Father's dark emotions. That LeRoy was "heard from all night," suggests

---

2 Fishberg, *Pulmonary Tuberculosis*, 565.

incessant coughing, and the plan to "take him North before long" shows the perceived gravity and urgency of his father's concern.

All of this would make perfect sense in light of a suspicion of childhood pulmonary tuberculosis—the white plague—as would the prescription of enforced rest four months later (May 4, 1857), once the diagnosis had been confirmed, possibly through multiple consultations.

That the rest cure was reapplied three years later in the context of back and leg pain, supports our strong suspicion that LeRoy was exhibiting the additional signs and symptoms of Pott's disease when he made the journey north to consult with Dr. Pancoast in Philadelphia in the summer of 1860.

Corset Support for Pott's Disease

Thursday February 5th 1863: ... Grandma made me a bandage that laces up + it is a great deal better than the other

LeRoy's grandmother devised a corset to support his back and provide an element of comfort in February, 1863.

In this context, it is interesting to note that plaster of Paris and aluminum corsets and steel braces were used to stabilize the progression of the spinal deformity in Pott's disease, and that the International Journal of Paleopathology reports skeletal changes associated with the use of traditional corsetry in a nineteenth century male with Pott's disease of the spine.[3]

The use of corsetry to buttress the slumping spine is further circumstantial evidence supporting a diagnosis of Pott's disease, and suggests that LeRoy may have suffered from the typical gibbus (hunchback) angulation of his spine that was so characteristic of the condition.

3   Moore, J., "The Use of Corsetry to Treat Pott's Disease of the Spine from 19th century Wolverhampton, England," in *International Journal of Paleopathology*, Vol. 14 (Sept. 2016), 74-80.

The Prescription of "Issues" and Peas
Erases All Lingering Doubt

*"Sunday June 24 [1860]: A bright and pleasant morn . . . Dr. Pancoast
came late at night and prescribed issues and lying down for the summer,
alas all the year."*

When Dr. Joseph Pancoast visited LeRoy in his Philadelphia hotel room on
the evening of June 24, 1860, he prescribed "issues and lying down for the
summer, alas all the year." The use of the word "issues" as something to be
prescribed is highly enigmatic to the modern medical mind—that is, until we
examine the writings of English surgeon Samuel Cooper, who devoted an entire
chapter of his 1809 surgical textbook to a discussion of Pott's disease, or
tuberculous spondylitis.[4]

Dr. Cooper begins by discussing the physical findings and diagnosis of
Pott's disease, including the paralysis that results from boney disintegration in
the spinal column:

> The paralytic affection of the legs is certainly owing to the particular state in which the
> spinal marrow, surrounded by the diseased vertebrae, is placed. When the distemper
> has existed only a short time the ligaments connecting the vertebrae, which form the
> curve, are somewhat thickened and relaxed, and the bodies of these bones affected with
> a change similar to what I have described as taking place in the heads of bones, in cases
> of white swellings. When the distemper has been of longer existence the ligaments are
> more manifestly thickened, and the bones more obviously altered, and even becoming
> carious [decayed, softened and porous].

The treatment of this condition, involved creating an issue—a suppurating,
or pus-draining lesion—on each side of the spinous processes by rubbing a
caustic substance on the skin, while protecting surrounding skin with an
adhesive plaster.

---

4   Cooper, Samuel, *The First Lines of the Practice of Surgery: Being an Elementary Work
   for Students, and a Concise Book of Reference for Practitioners . . .* (Justin Hinds, 1815),
   391-396.

The best mode of forming the issues is to rub the *kali purum cum calce viva* on the skin until the part turns brown. To accomplish this object in a neat manner it is as well to cover and defend the integuments by adhesive plaster, excepting the two longitudinal portions, about half an inch broad, which are to be converted into eschars by the application of the caustic.

Salsola-Kali (Saltwort). *Wikipedia*

Kali purum was a strong caustic vegetable alkali (from Arabic, *al-kali* or *al-qaliy,* "ashes of the Saltwort" or potash) that was prepared by evaporating a gallon of the water of pure kali (also known as Saltwort and *Salsola*), a marine plant found on the coasts of southern Europe and the Mediterranean, to dryness, and then melting it by fire.[5] The salt was deliquescent, meaning that it became liquid by the absorption of moisture from the air, making it inconvenient to apply, unless it was combined with *calce viva* (quicklime, or calcium oxide). Topical application of the strong alkali (potassium hydroxide) destroyed tissue by abstracting moisture.[6] It was intended to create a deep chemical burn, causing the skin and subcutaneous tissue to slough, leaving an ulcer through which matter could escape, or "issue," from the infected spine.[7]

---

5 T. Boardman, *A Dictionary of the Veterinary Art: Containing All the Modern Improvements* . . . (London, 1805).

6 D. M. R. Culbreth, *Manual of Materia Medica and Pharmacology* (Philadelphia, New York, 1896), 607.

7 Caustic issues have been in use since the time of Hippocrates. The early Greeks and Roman physician Celsus made them with a hot iron. The Egyptians and some Arab horsemen used "ustion" (the act of burning), igniting a rag or a candle wick on the site. Practitioners in China and Japan put lint or moxa on the skin and burned it to ashes. The Arabs, who liberally used the technique, frequently employed a chemical caustic. All used various dressings to keep the sore running until the underlying disease process was relieved or cured. The persistence of the ulcer was thought to be crucial to the success of the treatment. Hippocrates used issues in various conditions, including gout, sciatica, chronic disease of the lungs, liver and spleen, and scrofulous conditions of the joints. Roman physician Celsus, who lived during the time of Christ, recommended their use in diseases of the joints and phthisis (tuberculosis). John Eberle and H. W. Ducachet, *The American Medical Recorder*, Vol. 5. (Philadelphia), 1822, "On Caustic Issues," 216-224.

Medical Peas

"January Monday 21 [1861]: Today is Father's birthday. The peas were taken out of the issue this morning preparatory to healing up."

Remarkable events of Vol. II . . . "Jan 21 Peas taken out my back"

Once the initial application of caustic was finished, the protective plaster was removed and the wound covered with a linseed poultice. When the eschar of dead black skin began to separate from underlying tissue, a necklace-like array of dried peas or kidney beans on a string was placed into the cavity and covered with an adhesive plaster that was held in place with a tight bandage.[8] The idea was to maintain the tract and to suppress the formation of granulation tissue (proud flesh) that would necessitate the application of powdered cantharides (an irritant prepared from the dried bodies of the Spanish fly) or painful reapplication of the original caustic agent. The goal was to keep the "issue" open until the patient was cured, as evidenced by resolution of paralysis.

The fact that Dr. Joseph Pancoast prescribed "issues" in June 1860, and that LeRoy mentions "peas taken out my back" on January 21, 1861, is compelling evidence he was suffering from Pott's tuberculous spondylitis from his earliest days as a diarist, and that his physicians were fully aware of his diagnosis, and conversant with state-of-the-art treatments. It remains unclear how much of this information they shared with their young patient. He did not know he was terminally ill, although suspected as much when, on June 9, 1865, he dictated to his heart-broken mother, "I am perhaps [dying]," his mother unable to write the final word or words. He finally learned he was dying the day before his death.

The sad truth is that LeRoy comfort, vigor, and vitality were slowly being consumed by the "white plague" throughout the period of his writing, unbeknownst to him. His journal serves as a window into a Southern teenager's perspective on politics and the Civil War, as well as an in-depth chronicle of the suffering of one afflicted by the most pervasive pestilence of the day.

---

8   While a common dried garden pea was probably used in LeRoy's case, various other types of "peas" could also be employed, ranging from orange seeds, to glass or wooden beads, to balls of yellow wax compounded with caustic ingredients such as verdigris, orris powder, Spanish flies and white hellebore. *Cyclopedia of Practical Receipts in all the useful domestic arts, by a practical chemist, member of several scientific societies, etc., etc.* (London, John Churchill), 1841, 130.

4

The Natural History of Tuberculosis

Tuberculosis is a contagious disease, spread by the aerosolization of bacteria when a person with active disease coughs, sneezes, speaks, spits, laughs or sings. Dissemination usually requires close physical contact. Exposure to tuberculosis was widespread in nineteenth-century America. As much as 80% of the population may have been infected, most commonly during childhood. Most individuals showed no symptoms because their immune systems succeeded in controlling the growth of the microorganisms, forcing the infection into a latent or dormant phase. In situations where this did not occur, or where immunity was subsequently compromised, the disease emerged to advance relentlessly, often resulting in the death of its host.

Primary tuberculosis refers to a new infection in an individual whose immune system has never encountered the causal mycobacterium. Typically, the only symptom is a low-grade fever lasting for 2-3 weeks. The immune systems of most patients are able to arrest the replication of the bacillus, which then enters a dormant or latent phase. Only ten percent of individuals develop active tuberculosis pneumonia or distant dissemination from the primary exposure. Today, in this country, 10-15 million residents are thought to harbor latent tuberculosis.

Reactivation occurs when there is an attenuation of the immune system that allows latent bacilli in previously exposed individuals to begin to multiply again. Symptoms are progressive. Low-grade fever becomes more pronounced over time. It is classically diurnal and associated with night sweats. A nonproductive cough becomes more continuous and more productive. Nocturnal coughing is associated with advanced disease. Anorexia, wasting (consumption), and malaise are commonly seen in advanced stages. LeRoy Gresham exhibited symptoms and signs of advanced disease.

In modern times, we know that antimicrobial drug therapy is the only effective cure for tuberculosis. Typically, patients with active TB receive at least three drugs as their initial treatment. Using less than three agents can result in the development of resistant strains of the mycobacterium. The most common and effective anti-tubercular drugs include Isoniazid, Rifampin, Pyrazinamide, Ethambutol and Streptomycin. The course of treatment may last six months or more.

5

Pott's Disease

(Tuberculous Spondylitis; Spinal Caries)

Spinal tuberculosis is one of the oldest infirmities of mankind. Characteristic skeletal changes have been found in Egyptian mummies, and mycobacterial DNA has been recovered from human remains dating to the Iron Age.

The disease is popularly known as Pott's spine, in recognition of English surgeon Percivall Pott's seminal description, in 1779, of the typical progressive carious destruction of adjacent vertebral bodies, intervening disc space and other spinal elements, resulting in the hunchback spinal deformity and paralysis that are hallmarks of the condition. Pott did not specifically link the spinal anatomic changes with tuberculosis, although in further remarks three years later, he made references to an association of the condition with individuals of a strumous or scrofulous indisposition, to those with strumous tubercles in the lungs, and to individuals with enlarged, indurated and suppurating glands—classic features of scrofula, or tuberculous cervical lymphadenitis.

Spinal tuberculosis results when Mycobacteria enter the bloodstream, spreading from the lungs to the boney vertebral bodies. The anterior portion of the vertebra is usually affected first, with subsequent spread of the infection to the central body or disk, and to contiguous vertebrae. Multiple vertebrae are typically involved, usually in the lower thoracic or upper lumbar region. Anterior wedging results from the decay and collapse of the affected spinal elements, creating the characteristic gibbus deformity.

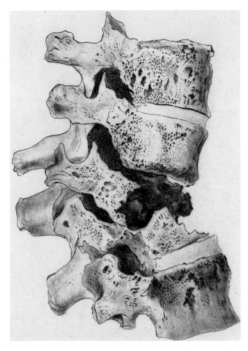

An example of a spinal column infected
with Pott's Disease.

The Chirurgical Works of Percivall Pott

Chronic back pain at the site of involvement is the most frequent symptom of spinal tuberculosis. The pain can be aggravated by movement of the spine, or by coughing or weight bearing.

Spinal TB can be associated with so-called "cold abscesses," which develop slowly as infection spreads into adjacent ligaments and soft tissues. These collections are not associated with the pain and intense inflammation that would be typical of suppurating bacterial infections. Bacterial superinfections may also develop within the disintegrating spine and soft tissues. Whether they be cold or hot, abscesses forming adjacent to the vertebral lesion in the paraspinal soft tissues are prone to track along fascial and ligamentous planes, and may cause pain at sites remote from the primary boney lesion.

The most devastating complication of spinal tuberculosis is paraplegia, which most typically results from impingement on the spinal cord by debris from decaying bone, pus or granulation tissue, or from subluxation and subsequent dislocation of the spine. Less common causes include tuberculous granulomas of the spinal dura, and infective anterior spinal artery thrombosis.[1] Neurological deficit occurs in up to three-quarters of patients with spinal tuberculosis. It usually begins as pain, weakness and numbness, often progressing to complete paralysis of one or both lower extremities.

1 Garg, R. K., "Spinal Tuberculosis: A review," in *Journal of Spinal Cord Medicine*, 34(5) (September, 2011), 440-454.

Another view of a disease-ridden
spinal column.

The Chirurgical Works of Percivall Pott

A Summary of the Observations of Percivall Pott on the Palsy of the Lower Limbs &c. (1779[2] and 1782[3])

English surgeon Sir Percivall Pott referred to the condition that bears his name as a palsy, marked by a total or partial loss of strength and movement in the lower extremities. This particular type of paralysis was associated with a characteristic outward curvature of the spine. Pott's initial impression was that the malady affected both sexes at all ages, but subsequent experience led him to conclude that it was primarily a disorder of weak and delicate infants and children. While adults were not exempt, he wrote that he never observed the condition in individuals beyond the age of forty.

2 Pott, P., "Remarks of that kind of palsy of the lower limbs, which is frequently found to accompany a curvature of the spine, and is supposed to be caused by it, together with its method of cure," in Earl, J., *The Chirurgical Works of Percivall Pott, F.R.S., Surgeon to St. Bartholomew's Hospital, A New Edition, with His Last Corrections , to Which Are Added A Short Account of the Life of the Author, A Method of Curing the Hydrocele by Injection, and Occasional Notes and Observations,* 3 Vols. (London, 1808), vol. 3, 233-256.

3 Pott, P, "Further Remarks on the Useless State of the Lower Limbs, in Consequence of a Curvature of the Spine, with some Observations of the Auxiliary Assistance of Mechanism, and other Remarks, by the Editor," in Earl, *The Chirurgical Works of Percivall Pott,* vol. 3, 259-296.

The onset of Pott's paralysis was gradual. The patient first became tired, languid, listless and unwilling to move about. This was followed by tripping, stumbling and involuntary crossing of the legs. The knees would give way, bending forward during standing, and the legs became largely insensate.

The condition differed from a common nervous palsy in that the legs and thighs were not rendered flaccid, but rather stiff—especially the ankles—resulting in a tonic extension of the legs, with downward pointing of the feet. The invariably outward curvature in the back produced a humped deformity and shortening of stature. Associated symptoms frequently included the loss of appetite, a hard dry cough, laborious respiration, pain and tightness in the stomach, a quick pulse, and a disposition to hectic (regular, recurrent fever). Erectile dysfunction and incontinence of feces and urine were not unusual.

Pott was intrigued by an observation that spontaneous drainage of an abscess near the spinal deformity of one of his teenage patients resulted in the restoration of the use of the boy's paralyzed limbs, leading him to suspect that a "distempered state" of the parts forming, or in the neighborhood of the curvature, preceded or accompanied it. In other words, there was a predisposing cause of the curvature.

The spinal curvature was invariably convex—from within outward. Postmortem examinations performed by Sir Percivall revealed thickening and laxity of the supporting ligaments of the spine, but the major disturbance seemed to be within the vertebral bodies. At first, he believed the changes were limited to an enlargement and spreading of the vertebrae. In the second edition of his work, however, he revised that opinion, stating that the problem was not so much enlargement, but rather carious erosion and destruction of the vertebral bodies and intervertebral cartilages. The spine bent forward, he surmised, as the result of the rotten bone giving way, as it became unable to bear the weight of the parts above.

In discussing the subject with one Dr. Cameron of Worchester, Pott learned that Hippocrates, the famous Greek physician of antiquity, had written of a cure of a patient with paralysis of the lower extremities after an abscess had developed on his back and spontaneously drained. Dr. Cameron had imitated this "act of nature" in his own practice by "exciting a discharge near the part"—an intervention that had proven very successful. Another surgeon in the community confirmed the effectiveness of the technique by repeating it.

Percivall Pott's first clinical experiment with such intervention involved the creation of an "issue" by making an incision on one side of the gibbus deformity on the back of an infant, and the placement of a pea in the opening. The child regained use of his legs within a month. His second experiment, performed on a 35-year-old man, involved the placement of a seton (a skein of cotton or other absorbent material passed below the skin as a stitch, and left with the ends protruding to promote drainage of fluid) on either side of the curve on the middle of the back. Within 6 weeks, the patient had recovered sensation in his legs and increased mobility. The procedure was repeated on a twelve-year-old boy who was totally helpless before treatment, but who regained the use of his legs.

Pott determined that "the remedy for this most dreadful disease consists merely in procuring a large discharge of matter, by suppuration, from underneath the membrana adiposa on each side of the curvature, and in maintaining such discharge until the patient shall have perfectly recovered the use of his legs." This could be accomplished by setons, by issues made by incision, or by issues made by a caustic. Pott preferred the latter because the technique was the least painful, least messy, and most easily manageable, in his personal experience.

Pott's technique involved making oval eschars approximately 1" x 3/4" on either side of the affected spine, taking care to maintain a sufficient portion of skin between them.

> The caustics should be applied on each side of the curvature, in such a manner as to leave the portion of skin covering the spinal processes of the protruding bones, entire and unhurt; and so large, that the sores upon the separations of the eschars, may easily hold each three or four peas in the case of the smallest curvature; but in large curves, at least as many more.

When the bottoms of the sores had become clean by suppuration, he would sprinkle a small amount of finely powdered cantharides (a preparation of powdered blister beetles, such as dried Spanish flies) every 3-4 days to prevent contracture of the wound edges, and to increase the discharge. As Pott wrote:

> These issues should not only be kept open, but the discharge from them should be maintained by means of orange peas, cantharides in fine powder, aerugo aeris, or any such application as may best serve the intended purpose, which should be that of a large, and long continued drain.

He kept the wounds open until the cure was complete, which he defined as perfect recovery of the use of the legs. He observed that cure of the palsy was not necessarily accompanied by the disappearance of the spinal curvature.

According to Pott:

> This and this only, does or can alleviate the misery attending the distemper, and in proper time effect a cure. By means of these discharges, the eroding caries is first checked, and then stopped; in consequence of which an incarnation takes place, and the cartilages between the bodies of the vertebrae having been previously destroyed, the bones become united with each other, and form a kind of anchylosis.

Pott stressed the importance of applying this remedy early in the course of disease. When this was done, he predicted it would be universally successful. If the bodies of the vertebrae had become completely carious and the intervening cartilages totally destroyed, however, no improvement was to be expected. The time required for successful completion of the cure varied with the extent of disease.

> No degree of benefit or relief, nor any the smallest tendency towards a cure, is to be expected until the caries be stopped, and the rotten bones have begun to incarn: the larger the quantity of bones concerned, and the greater degree of waste and havoc committed by the caries, the greater must be the length of time required for the correction of it, and for restoring to a sound state so large a quantity of distempered parts—and vice versa. I have seen it perfected in two or three months, and I have known it to require two years; two thirds of which time passed before there was any visible amendment.

Although the infectious microbial etiology of spinal tuberculosis was unknown in Percivall Pott's time, he did suspect an underlying causal agent, which he referred to as "a strumous or scrophulous indisposition."

> At the beginning of the preceding tract I have said . . . that there must certainly be either in the constitution of the patient, or in the state of the parts concerned, something which tended to produce this very dreadful malady.

> I am satisfied I was right in my conjecture, and am convinced, from every circumstance, general and particular, in the living, and from every appearance in the dead, that the complaint arises from what is commonly called a strumous or scrophulous indisposition, affecting the parts composing the spine, or those in its immediate vicinity.

Pott specifically associated the spinal curvature with strumous tubercles in the lungs and abdominal viscera:

These different affections of the spine, and of the parts in its immediate neighbourhood, are productive of many disorders, general and local, affecting the whole frame and habit of the patient, as well as particular parts; and, among the rest, of that curvature which is the subject of this inquiry; and it may not be amiss to remark, that strumous tubercles in the lungs, and a distempered state of some of the abdominal viscera, often make a part of them.

Pott specifically associated the spinal curvature with scrofula, or tuberculous cervical lymphadenitis:

The disease which produces these effects on the spine, and the parts in its vicinity, is what is in general called the scrophula . . . that same kind of indisposition as occasions the thick upper lip, the tedious obstinate ophthalmy, the indurated glands under the chin and in the neck, the obstructed mesentery, the hard dry cough, the glairy swellings of the wrist and ancles, the thickened ligaments of the joints, the enlargement and caries of the bones, &c. &c. &c.

English physician Charles Brown, writing in 1798, provided a contemporary definition of what Pott would have understood by his use of the term scrophula: a weakened action in the system manifesting itself by nine conditions, two of which included scrophulous tumors and ulcers (tuberculous lymphadenitis), and phthisis pulmonalis (pulmonary tuberculosis, or consumption).[4]

Through his association of the changes of spondylitis and paralysis with a scrophulous indisposition, with strumous tubercles in the lungs (pulmonary tuberculosis), with mesenteric obstruction producing a distempered state of the abdominal viscera, and with indurated glands under the chin and in the neck (scrofula), Percivall Pott was clearly placing the condition known as Pott's spine squarely within the spectrum of tuberculous illnesses, as they were understood in his time.

Jacques-Mathieu Delpech, chief surgeon of the Hôpital St. Èloi in Montpelier, France, referred to *mal du Pott* as *affection tuberculeuse des vertèbre in De l'Orthomorphie*, published in 1828.[5] For this, he is sometimes

---

4 Brown, Charles., "A Treatise on Scrophulous Diseases, Shewing the Good Effects of Factitious Airs: Illustrated with Cases and Observations" (M. Allen, 1798): http://tei.it.ox. ac.uk/tcp/Texts-HTML/free/K00/K008430.000.html.

5 Peltier, LF, *Orthopedics: A History and Iconography* (Norman Publishing, 1993).

credited as having been the first to establish an association of Pott's spine with tuberculosis. It seems clear, from a consideration of the historical record, that this is not the case.

Percival Pott himself had unambiguous inklings of such an association of his eponymous palsy with what we now understand to be tubercular disorders, forty-six years before Delpech set his thoughts on paper. In masterful style, Pott astutely and accurately described the clinical syndrome, introduced an effective (albeit not a curative) treatment, and intuited the existence of a common underlying cause of the spinal malady and a host of disturbances in other body systems. He deserves full credit for his comprehensive and ground-breaking work on the subject of tuberculous spondylitis.

6

"Saw Off My Leg"

Three times, on April 11, 1861, July 25, 1861 and December 22, 1862, LeRoy pathetically scrawled in his journal "Saw off my leg." On one occasion, he mentioned that the leg was "worse than ever," but the other two insertions are seemingly random.

During the Civil War, amputation was an operation that was commonly performed by both Union and Confederate surgeons. Undoubtedly LeRoy had encountered amputees within his local community, and he would have had some sense of the degree of handicap that was associated with the loss of a limb. Nevertheless, his suffering apparently was such that he contemplated this drastic solution more than once.

One of his recurring complaints was leg pain:

Thursday December 12 [1861]: . . . My leg pained me all night and I did not sleep well at all.

Tuesday April 8th 1862: . . . My leg pains me just enough to keep me awake at night.

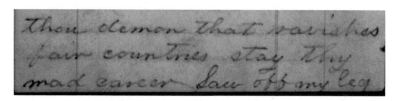

An entry from LeRoy's diary, April 11, 1861. *Library of Congress*

An example of a child's crutch. LeRoy was fitted for a similar crutch, and was also pulled in a small custom wagon.

Center for the History of Medicine, Harvard

Friday October 24th 1862: . . . My leg pained me and my cough worried me last night and this morn my right leg, my only good leg, is slightly contracted.

11th Nov. 1862 Teusday[1]: . . . my leg pained me more than it has since the time of Presbytery. . . . My leg is worse drawn up than ever before. . . .

Certainly chronic leg pain might have provoked LeRoy's drastic request; but other factors could have been at work as well. Percivall Pott described the rigidity and spasticity associated with the disease that bears his name:

> . . . the muscles . . . are rigid, and always at least in a tonic state [a state of continuous tension], by which the knees and ancles acquire a stiffness not very easy to overcome. By means of this stiffness, mixed with a kind of spasm, the legs of the patient are either constantly kept stretched out straight, in which case considerable force is required to bend the knees, or they are by the action of the stronger muscles drawn across each other in such manner as to require as much to separate them: when the leg is in a straight position, the extensor muscles act so powerfully as to require a considerable degree of force to bend the joints of the knees; and when they have been bent, the legs are immediately and strongly drawn up, with the heels toward the buttocks: by the rigidity of the ancle-joints, joined to the spasmodic action of the gastrocnemii muscles, the patient's toes are pointed downward in such manner as to render it impossible for him to put his foot flat to the ground; which makes one of the decisive characteristics of the distemper.

The pesky stiffness must have been extremely frustrating, and it is easy to see how his leg's interference with movement and positioning in his bed or in a chair or wagon might have prompted LeRoy to think it would be better if he were rid of it altogether.

---

1   LeRoy frequently misspelled this day of the week during the early years of his diary.

7

LeRoy's Doctors and
Medical Care During the Civil War

The world of medicine in the mid-nineteenth century was far different from the sophisticated technology-driven system we take for granted today. Then, there were no prerequisites for entry into medical schools. The medical curriculum consisted of only two years of study, with lectures being conducted only four or five months of each year. The curriculum for the second year was a repetition of the coursework from the first term. Clinical experience was not part of the program. There were no licensing boards. The germ theory of disease was unknown. There was no concept of sterility or antisepsis. Sanitation was not a major concern. Intravenous fluids did not exist. Anesthesia was in its infancy, consisting of chloroform or ether inhalation, introduced less than fifteen years previously. Medicines were largely plant or mineral based, and most physicians compounded their own drugs.

The relatively primitive state of affairs within the medical profession notwithstanding, physicians of the nineteenth century by and large possessed keen powers of observation, and they seem to have been motivated by the same desires that drive modern healers—to link causes with effects, and to relentlessly persevere in their search for solutions to the problems of human suffering.

LeRoy Gresham's Doctors

We do not have a detailed description of the full extent of the injury that initiated LeRoy's troubles, or of the treatment administered by local physicians during the first four years of his disability. All we know is that his physical condition was less than satisfactory, and that, as the diary opens, LeRoy's father had arranged to take him on a journey by rail and ship of over 800 miles to consult with a nationally recognized medical expert, and our suspicion is that this medical pilgrimage may have had more to do with his tuberculosis than with the traumatic injury.

During the Civil War years, the American South was largely a rural setting, especially when compared with major population centers of the North. With slightly over one million inhabitants, the entire state of Georgia had fewer residents than combined population of just two of the Union's leading cities, New York and Philadelphia.

LeRoy's hometown of Macon (pop. 8247) ranked fifth among the Georgia municipalities, behind Savannah (pop. 22,292), Augusta (pop. 14,493), Columbus (pop. 9,621) and Atlanta (pop. 9554). The state capital in Milledgeville, 30 miles northeast of Macon, had a mere 2480 residents.

In 1860, the state of Georgia could claim four medical schools—the Medical College of Georgia, established in 1829, and three rival institutions that had only recently sprung into existence, Savannah Medical College (1853), Atlanta Medical College (1855) and Oglethorpe Medical College (1856).

While there is no indication the Greshams lacked confidence in their local physicians, they apparently thought the time had come to use their considerable means to seek out the best available care for their ailing son. The moment must have been filled with expectation and hope as LeRoy's mother presented him with a new journal in which he could record the details of the medical and travel adventures that lay before him.

The purpose of the journey to Philadelphia was to consult with Dr. Joseph Pancoast, a distinguished general and plastic surgeon who held the chair of General, Descriptive and Surgical Anatomy at Jefferson Medical College. He was the author of A Treatise on Operative Surgery (1844), as well as of numerous other scholarly articles and books, and was highly regarded for his lectures and clinics in anatomy and surgery. Surely if anyone could provide the miracle that was needed, it would be this eminent specialist.

Sadly, the initial entries reveal that after less than a week in Philadelphia, the young patient and his father were on their way back from the northern medical Mecca with little more than a few encouraging words, a new prescription and instructions to rest. The secession of the Southern states and initiation of hostilities between the North and the South, made the logistics of continued contact between the Georgia youth and his Pennsylvania specialist significantly more difficult, and in practical fact, impossible. After January 1861, when Dr. Pancoast dispatched two bottles of medicine to LeRoy via express mail, there is no further mention of Dr. Pancoast in the journals.

Fortunately, a group of competent Philadelphia-trained medical practitioners was available in Macon and its vicinity. Dr. Edmund Fitzgerald enters the narrative in April, 1862. Having graduated from the Jefferson Medical College in 1848, he had spent the first six years of his professional life in Houston County, Georgia, relocating to Macon in 1854. According to his 1886 obituary, "he enjoyed the full confidence and respect of the community, and did a large and extensive practice among the best people of Macon."

In May, 1862, LeRoy was being attended by a Dr. White of Milledgeville, then the state capital of Georgia. Several prominent physicians named White were living in Milledgeville at the time. Dr. Benjamin Aspinwall White (1793-1866), a graduate of Harvard, had done his medical training in Philadelphia. He was president of the Georgia State Board of Physicians for most of his career, and was appointed Surgeon General of the Georgia State Troops in 1861. His son, Dr. Samuel Gore White (1824-1877), a graduate of the 1845 class of Jefferson Medical College in Philadelphia, served as Assistant Surgeon in the U. S. Navy until the close of the Mexican War, was mayor of Milledgeville in 1853-54, and was Surgeon in Cobb's Legion, 64th Georgia Infantry, during the Civil War.

Dr. William Scherzer, who treated LeRoy in September, 1862, had emigrated from Bavaria to Savannah, Georgia. He went on to study medicine at Hahnemann Medical College of Philadelphia, graduating in 1857, and then continued his training abroad in Vienna, Prague and Leipzig. Upon returning to the United States, he set up a medical practice in Macon, Georgia, where he stayed for several years before moving back to Savannah in 1866, and then on to New York two years later.

Based on the credentials and experience of his physicians, it appears that young Gresham had access to state-of-the-art medicine, as it was practiced in both the North and the South during the Civil War era.

8

LeRoy Gresham's Pharmacopoeia

Medicine, as practiced during the Civil War, lacked a modern scientific basis. The causes of many diseases were unknown. Medicines employed by nineteenth century physicians were largely plant or mineral-based. Many of them were used to treat multiple symptoms, but it is interesting to note how many of LeRoy Gresham's medicines were specifically employed in the treatment of tuberculosis.

Alcohol (Brandy, Porter, Whiskey, Catawba Wine)

Alcohol was used medicinally in the nineteenth century, both as a stimulant, to increase the cardiac output and blood pressure, and as a depressant and sedative. Because it could supply up to 40% of a patient's required calories and was easily absorbed, alcohol was also used as a calorie source for invalids.

Although alcohol abuse is now considered as a risk factor for

Vitis vinifera—the common grape vine.
Köhler's Medizinal-Pflanzn (1887)

tuberculosis, there was a belief among some physicians of the nineteenth century that alcohol was specifically antagonistic to tuberculosis.

Alum Water

Rockbridge Alum water was obtained from a mineral spring near Lexington, Virginia, and was endorsed for people afflicted with scrofula (tuberculous infection of the lymph nodes of the neck), incipient consumption (early stages of tuberculosis) and other pulmonary disorders including chronic forms of bronchitis, laryngitis and, pneumonia.

Belladonna

Belladonna, also known as Deadly Nightshade, is a perennial plant in the same family as the tomato, potato and eggplant. Atropine, scopolamine and hyoscyamine can be extracted from its foliage and berries. LeRoy used the drug as a plaster (medicine-filled gauze applied to the skin) for local pain relief and muscle relaxation.

Belladonna disrupts the parasympathetic nervous system. The window between therapeutic and toxic levels of the drug is quite narrow, and LeRoy may well have experienced significant side effects including dilatation of the pupils (with associated light sensitivity and blurred vision), rapid pulse, loss of balance, headache, flushing, urinary retention, dry mouth, constipation, confusion, hallucinations, delirium or convulsions.

In modern times, Belladonna can be obtained without a prescription at local pharmacies in ointments and plasters for use in the treatment of rheumatism, sciatica, and neuralgias. Atropine is used in

Atropa Belladona (Nightshade).
Köhler's Medizinal-Pflanzn (1887)

eye drops to produce pupil dilatation for ophthalmological examinations, and to accelerate an abnormally slow heart rhythm. Scopolamine patches are used to prevent nausea and motion sickness. The combination of belladonna and opium has been used for treatment of diarrhea and some forms of visceral pain, including bladder spasm. The combination is still available for use primarily in urologic practices as B&O suppositories.

Bismuth

Bismuth subsalicylate, and antidiarrheal agent, is the active ingredient in Pepto-Bismol and Kaopectate.

Creosote

Creosote was obtained by the distillation of coal and wood tar. It was suggested as a treatment for tuberculosis as early as 1833, and was recommended specifically for the control of coughing.

Dover's Powder

Dover's powder, a traditional medicine used for cold and fever, was developed by Thomas Dover, an eighteenth century English physician whose privateering voyage to the South Seas in the early 1700's provided the storyline for the novel Robinson Crusoe. The powder was a combination of ipecac (an agent to produce vomiting and expectoration), opium and potassium sulfate that was intended to induce sweating and prevent the development of a "cold" at the beginning of any attack of fever. It was also employed as a cough suppressant, antidiarrheal, and pain reliever, due to its opium component.

Hypophosphite of Lime

Hypophosphite of Lime was made by boiling phosphorus with lime, a calcium-containing mineral. The solution was then filtered and evaporated over sulphuric acid. The Compound Syrup of the Hypophosphites of iron, lime, soda and potassa was specifically hyped as "the best and the most rational of all remedies against consumption (tuberculosis)" and was advertised as a cure for tuberculosis.

Datura Stramonium (Jimson Weed).
Köhler's Medizinal-Pflanzn (1887)

Iodine

Iodine was widely used as a disinfectant, but it was also applied topically in the nineteenth century for the relief of the chest pain of tuberculosis.

Jimson Weed

Jimson weed or Devil's snare is another plant in the nightshade family, similar to Belladonna. It was used as a sedative, as a treatment for cough, intestinal cramps and diarrhea, and as a pain killer for arthritis, rheumatism and headache.

Lavender

The aromatic herb lavandula, or lavender, is widely thought to relax the nervous system, reduce stress, repel bugs, and encourage a good night's sleep.

Lavandula (Lavender).
Köhler's Medizinal-Pflanzn (1887)

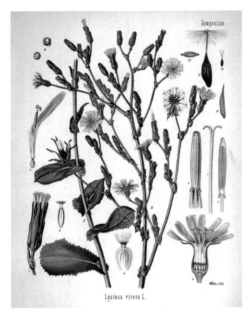

Lactuca Virosa (Lettuce).
Köhler's Medizinal-Pflanzn (1887)

Lettuce Opium

The milky fluid, or latex, secreted from the base of the stems of several species of lettuce was used as a sedative for irritable cough and as a sleeping aid for insomnia.

Mercury

Blue mass was a mercury-based medicine in pill form that was used in the nineteenth century as a treatment for syphilis, and as a remedy for tuberculosis, constipation, toothache, parasitic infections and the pains of childbirth.

Calomel (mercury chloride) was commonly used as a laxative.

Black wash referred to a lotion of calomel and limewater that was applied to syphilitic and other sores.

Mercury is very toxic. Symptoms of mercury poisoning could include muscle weakness, poor coordination, paresthesias (numbness in the hands and feet), rashes of the skin, anxiety, memory problems, trouble speaking, or difficulty with vision or hearing.

Magnesium citrate

Magnesium citrate is a saline laxative. LeRoy may have used it to treat constipation resulting from the use of belladonna derivatives and narcotic agents such as opium (including Dover's powder) and morphine.

Mustard Plaster

Mustard plasters were made by spreading mustard seed or powder inside a wet dressing. An enzymatic reaction in the wet mustard powder produced a

Brassica Nigra (Black Mustard).
Köhler's Medizinal-Pflanzn (1887)

chemical that was absorbed through the skin, providing warmth and stimulating nerve endings to distract the pain-sensing mechanism of the body. The warm dressing was used to treat rheumatism, arthritis and aching muscles. It was also prescribed for chest congestion. If left in place for too long, a mustard plaster could produce first-degree burns.

Opium

Opium latex, obtained from the opium poppy, contains the powerful pain-reliever, morphine, as well as the closely-related opiates codeine and thebaine (a precursor to synthetic opioids hydrocodone and hydromorphone).

Laudanum, was a "tincture of opium," a solution in ethanol, containing almost all of the opium alkaloids, including morphine and codeine.

While opium was used primarily as an analgesic, it had multiple roles in the pharmacopeia of the Civil War era. Due to its constipating effect, it became one of the most effective treatments for cholera, dysentery, and diarrhea. As a cough suppressant, opium was used to treat tuberculosis, bronchitis

Papaver Somniferum (Opium Poppy).
Köhler's Medizinal-Pflanzn (1887)

is a much adulterated article.
No. 8D420   Price, per 1-pound box............10c

Laudanum.
(Tinct. Opium.)
U. S. P. Strength. Directions on each bottle for young and old.
No. 8D424   Price
1-ounce bottle............ 8c
2-ounce bottle............15c
4-ounce bottle.............25c
Unmailable.

Paregoric.
Always useful, both for children and adults. One of the best known and most extensively used house remedies. Full directions.
No. 8D426 Price, 2-ounce bottle..10c
Price, 4-oz. bottle.................15c
It by mail, postage and tube extra, small, 12 cents; large, 16 cents.

Tasteless Castor Oil.

(Left) A typical ad for laudanum and Paregoric in a 1905 Sears catalog, demonstrating the easy accessibility and lack of regulation of narcotic pharmaceuticals in nineteenth-and early twentieth-century America.

Author

and other respiratory illnesses. Opium was additionally prescribed for insomnia. Compared with other drugs of the day, including mercury, arsenic and emetics, it was relatively benign, but had the potential for addiction.

Paregoric

Paregoric was a 4% opium tincture, also containing benzoic acid, camphor and anise oil. It was a household remedy in the 19th century, used to control diarrhea, and as an expectorant and cough medicine.

Pepper Tea

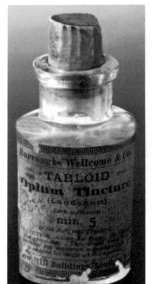

Black pepper was used to stimulate mucous production and loosen phlegm in patients suffering with a cough, sore throat or nasal congestion.

Quinine

Quinine, an alkaloid drug extracted from the bark of the cinchona tree, was specifically indicated for the treatment of malaria, but was used for the treatment of chills and fever of all kinds. Common side effects that LeRoy might have experienced from

A bottle of laudanum.
Wellcome Images, Science Museum, London

quinine were headache, ringing in the ears, and visual disturbances. More severe side effects could include deafness, low blood platelets, and an irregular heartbeat.

Sage Tea

Sage juice in warm water has been recommended since ancient times for treatment of hoarseness and coughs. Sage was officially listed in the United States Pharmacopoeia from 1840 to 1900.

9

Proprietary or Patent Medicines

Ad for Dalley's Pain Extractor,
"The great family ointment."

East Carolina Digital Collections

Dalley's Magical Pain Extractor

Henry Dalley established business as a merchant in New York City in 1839 introducing a medicinal concoction which he called Dalley's Magical Pain Extractor. The product met with little success at first, and Henry Dalley died disheartened in 1852. The business was taken over by Cornelius V. Clickener, wholesale druggist of New York City, who in 1855 published a 24-page booklet extolling the virtues of the Dalley's Magical Pain Extractor. Henry Daley Jr. assumed control of the firm in 1865, and the following year he introduced Dalley's Horse Salve (which was also promoted for use on cows, sheep, pigs and dogs).[1]

1 https://www.matchandmedicine.com/product/rs74b-dalleys-magical-pain-extractor-silk-paper/.

An advertisement for this medication appeared in *Great Metropolis* (1849, p. 169):

DALLEY'S MAGICAL PAIN EXTRACTOR

The Original and only Genuine. Facts are Stubborn Things. If you want the genuine article, apply at the Proprietor's only Depot in this city, 415 Broadway. No compound has ever been discovered that possesses any of the qualities of this famous remedy. Its infallibility is established as a remedy in the worst cases of Burns and Scalds, Piles, Rheumatism, Inflammations, Wounds, Sores, Cuts, Sprains, Swellings, &c. It extracts the pain almost instantaneously with its application, and heals the sores . . . wounds rapidly and without scar. MARK THE DIFFERENCE: The Genuine Dalley Extractor, when applied, cools and affords almost instantaneous relief; whereas the counterfeit and spurious Extractors irritate and increase the pain. Notice. —H. Dalley is the inventor of this invaluable remedy, and never has, and never will communicate to any living man the secret of its preparation. All Extractors, therefore, not made and put up by him, are base and vile counterfeits.

Dr. Spencer's Vegetable Anti-Bilious and Anti-Dyspeptic Pills

Dr. Spencer's Pills were essentially a popular vegetable laxative, although they were touted to cure for a host of ailments:

It is well known that diseases often arise from a foul and disordered state of the stomach and bowels; and if this condition is promptly attended to and relieved, that health will be immediately restored. And nothing more effectual can be resorted to than two or three good active doses of purgative medicine; and there is nothing more suitable than pills of a proper character. The public have in these vegetable pills the article presented to them, which possesses the equalities calculated to render the most important service in cleansing the alimentary canal; they will operate with sufficient force, and still with ease and safety; there is no ingredient in them that will render them dangerous as in taking cold, or cause any particular care in diet necessary. They have been used by the proprietor with abundant success in an extensive medical practice for many years. —He can therefore confidently recommend them to the public patronage. It is not vainly pretended that they will cure all diseases, but they will answer the purposes for which they are offered as well as any purgative medicine that can be produced; and by being taken when that description of medicine is needed, may save a person from threatened disease at a very small expense and without loss of time. A person can take them without any interruption of his customary employment.

Price only 25 cents a box.

Dr. J. F. Churchill's Compound Syrup of the Hypophosphites

Dr. J. F. Churchill, a specialist at a hospital for tuberculosis in London, presented a communication to the French Academy of Medicine in 1858, promoting the Hypophosphites of Lime and Soda for the treatment of consumption.[2] His theory was that tuberculosis originated from a deficiency of oxygen in the tissues. He proposed the use of hypophosphites as agents to enhance tissue oxygenation, based on the fact that phosphorus exists in a lower oxidation state than phosphate.[3] Churchill believed that the hypophosphites of lime and soda were best suited for insuring the absorption and assimilation of the proper form of the element. The hyperphosphite of lime, he thought, also had benefits in certain special cases.

Ad for Churchill's Syrup of Hypophosphite of Lime
Boston Medical and Surgical Journal, 1876

2   Churchill, J. F., *De la Cause Immediate et du Traitement Specifique/de la Phthisie Pulmonair et des Maladies Tuberculeuses* (Librairie de Victor Masson, 1858).

3   *Journal of Food Protection*, vol. 53, No. 6 (June 1990), 513-518.

On the basis of Churchill's theory, hypophosphites were used extensively in pharmaceutical preparations, even though reports soon began to appear claiming they were absolutely worthless in the treatment of tuberculosis.[4]

The Compound Syrup of the Hypophosphites, composed of the hypophosphites of iron, lime, soda and potassa, was marketed as Dr. Churchill's Specific Remedy for Consumption. Touted as a practical cure for tuberculosis, it created a major flash of optimism on the medical and pharmaceutical scenes in the early 1860's, both in Europe and in North America.

Dr. Jackson's Compound Syrup of the Phosphates or Chemical Food

Tuesday December 30th 1862: I got up last night and had a midnight coughing spell. Father bought me a new medicine a Syrup of Hyper-Phosphate, a sort of chemical food recommended by the celebrated Dr. Jackson of Philadelphia. It will do to take until I can get a supply of Dr. White's medicine, as mine is nearly out.

Interestingly, as Professor Churchill was promoting his Compound Syrup of Hypophosphites as a specific remedy for consumption, a medical entrepreneur in Philadelphia, Dr. Jackson (deviser of a popular cough syrup) was simultaneously introducing the Compound Syrup of the Phosphates, containing the phosphates of iron, lime, soda and potassa, as a treatment for weak bones and bow leggedness in children. [5]

Dr. Jackson's chemical bone food eventually was proven not to work for its intended purpose of preventing or correcting bow leggedness, and it faded into oblivion. It was never intended as a treatment for tuberculosis. However, the names of the ingredients in Churchill's and Jackson's syrups were eerily similar—iron, lime, soda and potassa. The difference was that one compound consisted of a group of phosphites ($H2PO2$), and the other, of phosphates ($H3PO4$). The one was made up of salts of phosphorous acid, or phosphinic acid; the other, salts of phosphoric acid. It is easy to get hyper-'s and hypo-'s

---

4   Cleaveland, C. H., ed., "Churchill's Hypophosphites in Phthisis," *Journal of Rational Medicine*, vol. I, No. 7 (July, 1860), 220.

5   Felter, H.W., ed., "New Remedies," in *The Eclectic Medical Journal*, Vol. 76, (January to December, 1916), 512-513.

and –phite's and –phate's mixed up, especially if one is not a chemist. Even today, mistakes are frequently made in prescribing and administering medications that sound and/or look alike. The confusion accounts for the innocent substitution of the celebrated Dr. Jackson's Bone Food by his father when LeRoy temporarily ran low on his prescription for Hyperphosphite Potassae on that December night in 1862.

10

Psychological Considerations

Addiction: Opium and Alcohol

A modern reader might wonder how a nineteenth-century teenager managed to maintain mental discipline and focus on a regular regimen of opium-derived medications (including Dover's powder, laudanum, and paregoric) and alcohol.

Modern theories of addiction suggest that pain offsets the euphoria otherwise produced by opioids. Without excess euphoria, the reward system is not triggered, and addiction does not develop so readily. "Users" in our modern culture do not have the physical pain to negate their euphoria. They pursue the "rush" of narcotics, becoming increasingly enslaved to it, eventually blunting their intellects, curiosity and motivation in the process. Leroy was simply interested in getting relief from his pain or cough, which never fully happened. His intellectual capacity seems to have been relatively unimpaired by the drugs, except for temporary physiological effects of doziness or "swimming" in his head while he was directly under their influence.

Fatal Depression

As the end of his life drew near, LeRoy had ample reason to be depressed. Besides the chronic cough, the painful back, draining abscesses, and paralyzed legs, he was suffering from gastrointestinal manifestations of TB—dyspepsia, ulcers in his throat, and diarrhea. Not only that, Lee's Army of Northern Virginia had surrendered to the Union at Appomattox on April 9, 1865. The

Confederacy's days were definitely numbered. Union flags were going up in honor of the subjugation of the South. There was a bounty on the head of President Jefferson Davis. Financial reverses were threatening to rock the stability of the formerly-affluent Gresham family. LeRoy was cut off from some of the people that he knew and loved, as well as from news of the outside world:

April 30, 1865. Dr. Hall called to see me this morning and examined my back + the abscesses. He is afraid to trouble them but is going to make me some tonic pills and see if he cannot relieve the indigestion + Dyspepsia from which I constantly suffer. I feel very low spirited myself + want to take something.

May 4. At 1 O'clock today a salute of 200 guns was fired and the bell was toll'd at the same time—out of respect to Lincoln I suppose. A tremendous federal flag was raised in front of the Lanier House. All this in honor of the subjugation of the Confederate States. . . . I am very low-spirited now, I am so completely helpless with both legs contracted and one of them almost paralyzed from pain.

May 10. 100,000 dollars reward is offered for Pres. D[avis], Clem Clay, 51 and others as the instigators of Lincoln's murder. A Yankee trick to hang him. Vice President Stephens is arrested + thus down comes the iron screw on our powerless necks.

May 14. I have never been so weak and . . . low-spirited.

May 28. I am quite unwell today + feel very despondent.
Jun 8. Nothing definite from Bill as yet—doubtful whether I will ever see him again. I have read nothing at all for the last ten days and consequently know little of the outside world.

Into this environment of discouragement, melancholy descended, and all hope seemed to vanish. LeRoy's last entry in his chronicle of consumption, on June 9, 1865, was a feeble, whispered, heartrending, "I am perhaps . . . [dying]." The pen was silent for nine days, and then the prophetic utterance was fulfilled.

11

Postmortem Review

What ultimately claimed the life of young LeRoy Wiley Gresham? Certainly Mycobacterium tuberculosis deserves a lion's share of the blame. But LeRoy coexisted with his infection for more than eight years, and things didn't really take a severe turn for the worst until the last two months, following General Robert E. Lee's surrender at Appomattox.

Modern theories of disease postulate links between human psychology and physiology. Diseases such as cancer are now being studied through the lens of psychoimmunology. Researchers tell us that the persistent activation of the hormones of the hypothalamic-pituitary-adrenal axis in response to chronic stress or depression impairs the immune response and contributes to the development and progression of diseases such as cancer.[1] Specifically, depression is known to enhance the production of pro-inflammatory cytokines (IL-6) and to cause the down-regulation of cellular and humoral immune responses. Depressed and otherwise stressed individuals have slower and weaker immune responses to vaccines, are slower to develop immune responses to pathogens, have substantial delays in wound healing, and are at increased risk for wound infection after injury. In short, they show increased vulnerability to infectious disease and poorer recovery from infection.[2]

---

1 Reiche, E. M., Nunes, S. O., and Morimoto, H. K., "Stress, depression, the immune system and cancer," in *Lancet Oncol* October 5 , 2004), 10: 617-25.

2 Kiecolt-Glaser, J.K., and Glaser, R., "Depression and Immune Function: Central Pathways to Morbidity and Mortality," in *Journal of Psychosomatic Research*, vol. 53 (2002), 873-876.

The parallel demise of LeRoy Gresham and the Confederate South has intrigued me since I first became familiar with the diary. LeRoy was a son of the South, and he identified closely with its destiny. Although, as an invalid, he could not fight its battles, he reveled in its victories from the sidelines, and bemoaned its defeats. When the cause seemed all but lost, he seemed to give up too, becoming clinically depressed. There is good reason to believe, based on our current theories of the workings of the human immune system that, with this psychological capitulation, there was a corresponding surrender in the physical struggle of his body against the microbial invaders.

Having conceded the field, it was only a matter of days before the Mycobacteria could claim LeRoy's life as another trophy in their age-old contest with humanity.

A Chronicle of Consumption

The Medical Entries, with Commentary

The first indication we have in the historical record that LeRoy was ill and his parents knew it comes from a letter written by LeRoy's father, John Jones Gresham, to his wife Mary Eliza Baxter Gresham. It suggests that tuberculosis might have been suspected by LeRoy's doctors as early as January 1857, when the boy was only nine years old.[1]

Saturday night
Macon Jany 10/57

My dear Mary

Upon our return this afternoon from Houston I received your very welcome letter and read the readable parts of it to our dear boys who were delighted to hear from you.

I sent Howard off the day you left with my new overseer and we went down the next day to install him. I am afraid he is not much but it was the best I could do. Thomas enjoyed himself finely killing birds in which he was quite successful and poor Loy seemed happy + cheerful but was not disposed to take much exercise and remained mostly about the house and yard. He stood the ride home very well to day + sang + laughed nearly all the way, while my heart was aching with pain. I could think of little else and

---

1 LeRoy was born on November 11, 1847.

would often ride with my arms around him – pressing him to me – how little he or any but you knew what I felt.[2] When I lost my hurt boy in your absence – and such a boy – and how to break the news to you myself, I thought the trial severe, but this – who can tell the anguish – I can't write about it + yet I can write about nothing else. Perhaps I was wrong to say I was perfectly miserable. I have yet other blessings left for which I would not be ungrateful. But my poor boy!!

It was pretty hard work to keep warm last night, and the wind blew as it only blows on this hill + in our room. Thomas slept with me + LeRoy on Minnie's couch. He was heard from all night till was late before we had the courage to reach our toilette this morning.[3] Your hiding the wood house key compels us to burn very mean half rotten wood to day + I shall be compelled to buy some. There is however another way into the wood house – through the cellar.

PS I shall let Loy go to school in the morning but the Doctors wish to examine him again before giving their advice. I think I should take him North before long…[4]

Before it was determined that LeRoy had TB, it was widely speculated that his leg injury was the cause of all his woes. There is no indication within LeRoy's diary as to how he had injured his leg. However, as noted earlier in the Publisher's Preface, a newspaper account by Macon native Albert Martin Ayres many decades later recalled that his leg was crushed by a chimney collapse. "The little boy at my side had his leg all broken up," wrote Ayres, "and I think he was crippled until he died.[5]

With these considerations in mind, the following excerpted medical comments from LeRoy's diary, together with medical commentary, can be understood in context with how LeRoy was experiencing his disease and injury. It is important to remember that he did not know he was suffering from TB.

2   LeRoy is happy, cheerful, singing and laughing, but his father is overwhelmed with profound grief and foreboding. Something more ominous is afoot.

3   That LeRoy was "heard from all night," suggests incessant coughing, a symptom of pulmonary tuberculosis.

4   The plan to "take him North before long" emphasizes the perceived gravity and urgency of his father's concern.

5   Gresham family letters and LeRoy's own pen date the accident to September 21, 1856. The full recollection, found in Smale, *Ayres Memoirs*, 8, is reproduced in Janet E. Croon, ed., *The War Outside My Window*, ix.

Volume 1
June 14, 1860 – March 26, 1861

On Thursday, June 14, 1860, LeRoy and his father bid farewell to mother, brother and sister, as each of them entered their signatures into his new journal. The following morning, father and son depart for Savannah, where they board the *State of Georgia*, a ship bound for Philadelphia, intending there to consult with the eminent Dr. Joseph Pancoast at the Jefferson Medical College. They pass Cape Hattteras on Sunday morning, arrive safely in the City of Brotherly Love on Monday June 18, at one in the afternoon, and check into the Continental Hotel. The diary spans a period of precisely five years from this point of highest optimism and expectation. LeRoy will draw his last breath on the anniversary of this day, June 18, 1865.

Teusday June 19: Went over to the Board of Publication rooms this morning and bought Luyman Hogue. It is a very nice little book indeed. In the evening, Dr. Pancoast[6] came up + saw me. He gave no decided opinion, but said he found me better than he expected. Father and I went round to the academy of Natural Science. It is a most wonderful place. There are birds and animals of all descriptions. There are also skeletons of all and about 500 skulls all on shelves.[7]

Friday June 22: Dr. Pancoast came to see me again to day and did nothing but prescribe a fourth medicine. I went round to the mint to day and excepting that have layed down most of the time.

Saturday June 23rd: I have not been out any but have layed down a most of the time. I can see a fire from the window but it don't seem to be a large one. Dr. Pancoast came to see me again this evening.

---

6 Dr. Joseph Pancoast (1805-1882) was a prominent Philadelphia surgeon and lecturer associated with the Jefferson Medical School and Hospital. He was known for many innovative procedures and is considered one of the first plastic surgeons. Howard Atwood Kelly, M.D., *A Cyclopedia of American Medical Biography: Comprising the Lives of Eminent Deceased Physicians and Surgeons from 1610 to 1920*, 2 vols. (W.B. Saunders Co., 1912), Vol. 2., 241-242.

7 Although it is very hot and he does not have much energy, LeRoy is apparently able to get around, visiting the Board of Publication and the Academy of Natural Science on Tuesday and the mint a few days later.

Sunday June 24: . . . Dr. Pancoast came late at night and prescribed issues and lying down for the summer alas all the year.[8]

After a stay of just one week, LeRoy and his father depart Philadelphia on the morning of June 25, traveling by rail and arriving in New York City about eight hours later. The following afternoon, they board a ship for Savannah, where they arrive on June 29 and take a train for Macon. It is an arduous trip for a sick boy.

Teusday Oct 9 1860: Went down to dentists and had a rousing plug put in. Also one on the 17 and 18 days of October.

November 11, 1860: My birthday and I have just recovered from a spell of sickness.

1861

Jan. 2nd: . . . My Back does not pain me except when it is being dressed. Two bottles of medicine came by express from Dr. Joseph Pancoast.

January 6th 1861: … I also am troubled with a pain in my hip.

January Monday 21: … The peas were taken out of the issue this morning preparatory to healing up.[9]

January 25 Friday [18]61: … My leg and back not improved much and give me a good deal of pain and trouble.

January 26, 1861: … My cough is no better.

Febuary 7, 1861: … Slept very poorly last night… My leg and back are no better but I hope they will improve soon.

Febuary 8th 1861: … My cough has been a great deal worse in the last two or three days.

Feb 8 1861: … I went on my wagon to day for the first time in 3 months.

Febuary 12 Teusday: … My cough is, I hope, a little better but my leg is no –

---

8   LeRoy's use of the term "issues" as something to be *prescribed* should arouse great curiosity in the minds of modern readers. Deciphering the meaning proved to be the key to unlocking the true nature and scope of his illness.

9   See the discussion of issues and peas in the treatment of Pott's disease of the spine on page 29.

Febuary 18 Monday: ... Uncle John came up to see me this evening.[10]

Thursday Feb 21: ... My back is not healed up yet and my leg is no better.

Feb 24 Sunday: ... My cough is very troublesome last night.

Monday 25 Feb: ... Was sick all night, coughed a great deal.

Feb 26 Teusday: ... Coughing almost incessantly.

March 2nd Saturday: ... My cough troubles me some though not so much as it has done. My issues have not healed up yet and it is over a month since they started.[11]

Sunday March 3: ... Uncle John came up to see us.

March 13 Wednesday: ... My back was dressed this morning and it is not healed up yet.

March 16 Saturday: ... My cough very troublesome indeed.

March 20 Wednesday: ... My back was dressed this morning and it beginning to heal. Sweet time about it.

Sunday March 24: ... I have a bad head ache to night and shall go to bed directly.

Volume 2
March 27, 1861 – August 1, 1861

March 27 Wednesday: ...Father brought up a bottle of Rockbridge alum water.[12] Not very nice.

Friday March 29 1861: ... Had a bad headache all night and did not sleep well.

---

10 John Springs Baxter was not only LeRoy's uncle, but also a local Macon physician.

11 The "issues" have not healed yet, on March 2, 1861, and it is over a month since they "started." The point to make here is that "started" does not signify a month since the "issues" were created. That procedure must have been performed much earlier. We don't know if Dr. Pancoast did it in Philadelphia, or if LeRoy's Macon physicians did it on his recommendation. In fact, the peas that were used to maintain the "issues" were *removed* on January 21, "preparatory to healing up" a little more than a month before this March 2 entry. After the peas were removed, the "issues" could begin to close. That process was incomplete six weeks later.

12 Mineral water from the Rockbridge Springs in Virginia. It was recommended for the treatment of consumption. See pages 10, 39.

Sunday March 31 1861: ... My leg don't get any better or any worse; neither does my cough.

April 3 Wednesday 1861: Coughed nearly all night and coughed nearly all morning. ... I got a letter from Dr. Pancoast today. ... Father bought me some Hore Hound candy today.[13]

April 4 Thursday 1861: ...Cough still troublesome.

Friday April 5 1861: ... Cough is troublesome.

Sunday April 7 1861: ... My cough is not so troublesome as it was.

April 8 Monday 1861: ... Cough a good deal better. Raining hard all morning.

April 11 Thursday 1861: My cough is considerably improved. Saw off my leg.

April 15 Monday: ... Back very nearly well.

April 16 Teusday: ... Uncle John came to see me this afternoon.

April 17 Wednesday: ... Head acked [ached] all day.

April 20 Saturday: Put a belladonna plaster on my back last night. ...

April 23 Teusday: ... My cough is some what worse. ... Did not sleep well on acct of the intolerable itching of the Belladonna plaster.

April 24 Wednesday: ... Had a very violent spell of coughing together with vomiting. ... Took a little morphin[e] last night and did not sleep well, consequently drowsy all day.

April 25th Thursday: ... Slept only with the aid of an opiate.

April 28 Sunday: ... I was very restless and did not sleep well.

April 29 Monday: ... Slept miserably last night.

May 1st Wednesday: ... My leg is in the same condition and I hope it will get no worse. Slept indifferently although I took opium Hyociamus and spirits of lavender.

May 6 Monday: I have had almost constant headache for the last two or three days...

May 8 Wednesday: ... My cough is pretty troublesome.

13 Horehound was an herbal candy often used to suppress coughing.

Monday May 13: ... My back was dressed this morning and it was not in a good condition. It ran a good deal and was very sore. One of them is entirely well.[14]

May 17 Friday: ... It is painfully dull for me these long summer evenings: Father and [others] go off and go to sleep and I can not do that.

Sunday May 19 1861: ... My appetite is very variable indeed. Sometimes better, again worse. For the last two or three days I have not had enough for a cat[15]. ... Father brought me a book Analysis of Rock Bridge Alum Water. If it does all the book says it must be a great thing.

May 21 Teusday 1861: ... I am coughing a good deal more than usual this morning.

Thursday May 23, 1861: ... I have slept a good deal better for the last week and hope to continue to do so.

Sunday May 26 1861: ... My back not well yet; they are putting Jinison Weed salve on it. My back it is not improved in the least although my General Health is remarkably good.

Monday May 27 1861: ... My appetite is a good deal better lately.

May 30 Thursday 1861: ... had awful headache all day and slept in the evening.

Monday June 3rd 1861: ... My back is very sore indeed now, and I wish it was well. ... My cough is improved.

Wednesday June 5 1861: ... My back is not healing hardly at all. I look but almost fear to do so. My leg is improving.[16] My cough is certainly improved a great deal.

June 8 Friday 1861: ... My back was dressed to day and shows few signs of healing. This is certainly a sore of the longest calibre I ever heard of.

Sunday June 9 1861: ... I feel truly bad, having had a very annoying and depressing headache all day.

June 10 Monday 10 1861: ... I have not entirely got over my headache yet.

---

14 Issues were commonly made on both sides of the affected vertebra, although not necessarily both at the same time. Apparently one has closed up, at least temporarily.

15 Anorexia is part of the wasting process that is responsible for the term "consumption" as a descriptive name for the disease we now know as tuberculosis.

16 The therapeutic goal of creating an "issue" was to relieve compression on the spinal cord and alleviate paralysis. Perhaps the treatment was having some success?

Teusday June 11 1861: My headache still continues and is very annoying. ... My cough has grown suddenly worse again, greatly to my sorrow. Have expectorated a great deal today.[17]

June 12 Wednesday 1861: Woke up with a headache again this morning. ... I am very sorry my back cough is worse.

June 13 Thursday: Fast day – Slept most bad last night, and feel as if I had been beat this morning.

Friday June 14 1861: ... I slept most miserably last night. ... I am free from a headache this morning, although I feel very bad.

Saturday 15 June 1861: I feel very drowsy and bad this morning, having taken a Dover's Powder[18] last night. I also cough a good deal.

Sunday June 16 1861: ... Took a Dover's Powder and slept very badly... I do not feel quite well yet, still having a lurking headache. ... My cough is a little better this morning.

Monday June 17 1861: ... I feel tolerably well today.

June 18 Teusday 1861: ... I slept better than usual.

Wednesday June 19 1861: ... Slept very well indeed for me. ... My back appears not to be healing at all. Put beeswax and tallow on it this morn, a concoction of Father's. I think my leg is better, and my cough is also improved again I hope.

June 21 Friday 1861: ... Aunt Eliza has been trying to persuade me to have my back burnt with caustic.[19]

Sunday June 23rd 1861: Another scorcher. I have never suffered more in heat in my life than I have in the last two or three days. ... Every body gone to Uncle Jack's funeral, leaving me lying in the passage. ... This time last year I was in Philadelphia, the headquarters of abolitionism, lodged in room 104 Continental

---

17 Coughing with expectoration of purulent sputum is a common sign of active pulmonary tuberculosis. The sputum was highly infectious.

18 Dover's Powder was a combination of the active ingredient in syrup of ipecac and opium, and used to treat conditions as wide-ranging as colds, dysentery, pain, insomnia, and coughing. Drowsiness could be an after-effect of the medicine.

19 Application of a caustic such as *kali purum cum calce viva* was one of the methods of making and maintaining "issues" in the treatment of spinal tuberculosis.

Hotel. I don't care about going there but I would like to see Dr. Pancoast.[20] I have slept tolerably notwithstanding the awfully hot weather.

Monday June 24 1861: … I wish my back was well, but I do hate to put caustic on it. Aunt Eliza has gone home.

Monday June 27 1861: … I have had a sort of crick in my neck for a day or so. I think I must have taken cold.

June 29 Saturday: I am very well except that every night I have a right decided fever[21] and consequently sleep bad. … My back heals awfully slow.

July 1st Monday 1861: … I took a dose [of] blue moss[22] last eve.

July 5 Friday 1861: … Back has not healed at all. I slept in a bed by myself, having slept with Mother for a good while. … Dressed my back today. … I have got a headache.

July 6 Saturday 1861: I have still got a headache.

July 8 Monday 1861: … Did not sleep well at all. Got some Dalley's Pain extractor [liniment] to put on my back today.

Friday July 12 1861: … My Back is no better.

Saturday July 13, 1861: … We have quit putting Dally on my back now. I am getting long very well except this. I do wish it would heal.

Macon July 15 1861: Have had a bad headache all day. … Put black wash on my back.[23]

July 17 Wednesday 1861: … My back shows no sign of healing and won't till caustic is put on it.

July 18 Thursday 1861: … My back was dressed and actually it has healed a little.

Friday July 19 1861: … I hope my back will be almost well by the next dressing.

---

20 The hostilities between the North and South make it impossible for LeRoy to continue his attachment to the Philadelphia specialist.

21 Fevers, chills and sweats are classic symptoms seen with infectious illnesses such as tuberculosis.

22 "Blue mass" was a compound used to treat several maladies, including syphilis and tuberculosis, containing about 1/3 mercury—a very toxic substance.

23 Consisted of glycerin and black oxide of mercury or nitrate of silver.

Saturday July 20 1861: Slept well. ...

Macon July 22 1861: ... Dressed my back this morning and its healing though very slowly.

Thursday July 25th 1861: ... My back is nearly well and I am very glad. ... "Saw off my leg" I had a headache all the morn and it is much better now.

Friday July 26 1861: ... My back is at last well.

Monday July 29 1861: ... I sleep most misbrally these nights tho.

Volume 3
August 2, 1861 – December 30, 1861

Saturday August 3 1861: ... I slept very badly. Mother was carrying me this morn + stumbled and fell hurting her knee.[24] It did not hurt me at all.

Thursday August 8 1861: ... I woke this morning with a sore throat but do not think it permanent.

Wednesday August 14: ... I have got a very bad headache.

Saturday August 17 1861: ... Got a bad headache today.

August 20 Teusday: ... Slight Headache today.

August 28 Wednesday: ... Mother brought me a large pear and a bottle of extra fine brandy from Mrs. Cobb.[25] Mr. Cobb imported it himself.

Friday August 30: ... I have had a bad headacke all day.

Sunday September 1st 1861: I slept with Thomas and for a wonder slept tolerably well.

September 11 Wednes.: . . . Arrived here safely with a scorching headache.

September 16 Monday: ... I have got a bad cold in the head and do not feel well at all.

Wednesday September 18: ... I have recovered entirely from my cold.

---

24 LeRoy must be very slight and frail for his mother to be able to carry him at the age of 13 years and nine months.

25 See the discussion of alcohol in the treatment of tuberculosis, pages 12-13.

Friday September 20: On this day 5 years ago my leg was broken and from that time I have never been altogether well[26]. … Father brought up some splendid Catawba wine yesterday …. Monday I have got a bad headache and did not rest well at all.

Sabbath day September 22: … Slept very badly last night. . ..

Friday September 27: … I do not feel well at all.

Sabbath day September 29: … Father got me some Horehound candy for my cough yesterday.[27]

Friday October 4th: … I have a very bad headache and did not sleep well at all.

Monday October 7th: … Yesterday was an awful day for me.[28]

Tuesday October 8th: … I am very tired tonight having been on my wagon nearly all day.

Friday October 18: … I did not sleep well at all. I had a very bad pain in my back and Mother put a mustard plaster on me over which I made a tremendous fuss.[29] … I am going to try to keep very quiet today and not get up at all. I expect that's what's the matter with my back now.[30] … My back pains me very bad.

Saturday October 19: … I slept none. The pain in my back was very bad; I took a Dover's Powder. . . . I have slept all the morning and have now got a headache This is the first morning I have stayed in the house for sickness in a long time. I hope it will be the very last one.

---

26 This entry dates the accident to September 20, 1856.

27 A hard candy made from the Horehound plant that tastes like licorice, mint, and root beer. It soothed throats and was believed to lessen coughs.

28 LeRoy often mentions his physical health in passing ("Yesterday was an awful day for me") before continuing on to other matters. A close reading of his entries demonstrates he suffered considerably more pain and general discomfort than he shared with his diary, from headaches (some almost certainly brought about by the various "medicines" and home remedies routinely served him) to lower back and leg pain, a wide variety of skin issues, and chronic coughing.

29 A mustard plaster is a poultice (soft, moist mass often heated) of mustard seed powder inside a dressing applied to the skin. The wet mustard powder produces a chemical (allyl isothiocyante) absorbed through the skin, providing warmth. The stimulation of the nerve endings eased pain.

30 LeRoy means he has been too active, and the activity has strained his back. Physicians in the nineteenth century believed that rest was a key element in the treatment of pulmonary and spinal tuberculosis.

Sunday October 20: ... I feel a good deal better. Mother is sick. Took some seltzer water. . .. The pain in my back is a little better.

Monday October 21: ... I slept very badly and I took a Dover's Powder. The pain in my back was very bad. ... The pain in my back is not so bad as last night.

Saturday October 26: ... I am very well.

Wednesday October 30: ... I have a headache tonight.

Thursday October 31: ... I stayed out doors all the morning; I have as yet had no sign of the return of my bad cough.

Sabbath November 3: ... I have got a slight sore throat this morn.

Monday November 4: ... I have had a bad cold in my head; my throat is a good deal better.

Saturday November 9: ... I have a bad pain in my back and took a Dover's Powder.

Sunday November 10: ... I feel very sleepy and bad today, having taken a Dover's Powder. The pain in my back is not improved and I am coughing very considerably.

Friday November 15: ... I feel very well today, and stayed on my wagon all the morning, shooting bow and arrow.

Teusday November 19: ... I have a headache this evening.

Monday December 2: ... I have had a very bad headache all day.

Teusday December 3: ... Got a headache still.

Friday December 6: ... I have got a pain behind my shoulder today.

Sunday Dec. 8: Grandma brought me a roll of tobacco from Eliza ... I feel just as well as I can today.

Thursday December 12: ... My leg pained me all night and I did not sleep well at all.

Friday December 13: ... I have got a distressing headache and I took a Dover's Powder last night.

Sunday December 15: ... The pain in my side has left me entirely.

Sunday December 22: ... I took a Dover's Powder on account of my leg.

Volume 4
January 1, 1862 – February 12, 1863

Saturday January 4th 1862: … I took a Dover's Powder and my leg hurts me now.

Sunday January 5th 1862: … Took a Dover's Powder. . . . My leg is much better.

Thursday January 9th 1862: … I have got a pain in my back and have had for several days.

Monday January 12th 1862: [sic] … I did sleep most miserably last night.

Teusday January 14th 1862: … My leg is drawn up a good deal this morning.

Friday January 17th 1862: … I have had a distressing pain in my hip point.[31] I wonder whether I am going to have hip disease…. I wish very much I could hear from Dr. Pancoast to know whether or not I am getting well.[32]

Saturday January 18th 1862: … I slept very miserably last night on acct of the terrible pain in my hip and back. Minnie was also sick. I had to take a Dover's Powder before I could rest at all. … I hope this pain in my leg is rheumatism.

Sunday January 19 1861: … I slept under the influence of a Dover's Powder tolerably well, though suffering a good deal. … Father rubbed my back with liniment last night.

Teusday January 21st 1862: … I spent a better night and my leg does not hurt me as bad.

Wednesday January 22nd 1862: … My leg is nearly well.

Tuesday February 4th 1862: … Father rubbed my back with liniment and it feels a good deal better this morn.

Monday February 17th 1862: … Had very considerable sore throat through the night and this morning.

Tuesday February 18, 1862: … My sore throat is entirely well.

---

31 The greater trochanter of the femur protrudes on the lateral aspect of the hip, and could be described as a "point." In addition to affecting the spine (Pott's disease), skeletal tuberculosis can also involve large joints, such as the hip.

32 His 1860 visit with Dr. Pancoast in Philadelphia was brief, but LeRoy liked him very much, trusted him, and hoped for good news and progress that would never come.

Friday February 21st 1862: … I have caught a bad cold in my head which worries me considerably. Snuf-Snuff.

Saturday February 22nd 1862 AD: … I took some pepper tea last night and my cold is a great deal better. … I have commenced to take Iron pills again.

Sunday February 23d 1862: … My cold, through the influence of pepper tea and a little care, has left me.

Wednesday February 26th 1862: … Have had a bad pain in my head all the eve and have coughed a good deal.

Wednesday March 5th 1862: … I did sleep most miserably.

Thursday March 6th 1862: … I slept very bad and got up at eleven AM.

Saturday March 8th 1862: … I have got my old pain in the back and hip. Had to take Dover's Powder. Rubbed my back with liniment.

Sunday March 9th 1862: … The pain in my back is gone, and I am well again. Father bought me a new supply of Catawba wine.

Monday March 10th 1862: … In turning a corner this morn very unexpectedly on my wagon [while being pulled], I was thrown off and received a severe jolt which did not hurt me at all at the time, but which I fear will be of no good to me.

Saturday March 22nd 1862: … I passed a most uncomfortable night in consequence of a pain in my hip.

Sabbath day March 23d 1862: … I have had my old troublesome enemy, the pain in hip and back, in full force today, and yesterday. Last night I took a Dover's Powder which gave me a quiet night and made me feel sleepy and bad today

Monday March 24, 1862: … Rubbed my back with liniment last night and took some brandy in going to bed, but did not go to sleep, and had to take a Dover's Powder. Today I am worse still. A constant, never ceasing, pain. No sleep at night, no rest in the day. It hailed very hard yesterday at 6 P.M. for a ¼ of an hour.

I enjoyed eating it very much and ran about a good deal which made my leg worse.[33] ... I lay on the floor in the eve, feeling stupid + sleepy.[34]

Teusday March 25th 1862: ... My hand trembles very bad and I am hardly able to write. I am a great deal easier today for which I am very thankful. I took a "Dover" and had my back rubbed. Slept until about 11½ A.M. at which fashionable hour I arose and partook of breakfast. I took one of Dr. Spencer's celebrated pills today.[35] Also some Seltzer. ... Jim Campbell came up to play chess with me, but my leg was too bad. It grows much worse toward night.

Wednesday March 26th 1862: ... Slept bad. Took a Dover's Powder and a Spencer's pill. This morn, I took two more pills and a dose of Seltzer.

Thursday March 27th 1862: ... Took a Dover's Powder last night. ... My leg still hurts me some.

Friday March 28th 1862: ... I slept very poor last night. My leg gave me a great deal of pain, although I took a Dover's Powder. ... Father put a Belladonna plaster on my back this eve.[36]

Saturday March 29th 1862: ... Spent a better night with the usual remedy and feel better today. ... Plaster is very comfortable. ... Have not got my lesson for over a week on account of sickness.

Sabbath day March 30th 1862: ... I slept very bad. My plaster itched all night so I had to take a Dover's Powder. It itches now. ... Took the plaster off tonight and it had drawn very much indeed.

Monday March 31st 1862: ... My back is better though it keeps me constantly scratching.

33 LeRoy could not run, so his use of the word "ran" should not be taken literally. He spent nearly all of his time lying down or reclined, but would very occasionally move about on his own. Being a young boy, he naturally tried to do more than he could or should. Three years after his injury, for example, his father warned him not to try and slide on ice (letter to Mary Gresham, dated Jan. 19, 1859). A hail storm was rare, and on this day he went outside (surely with help) and moved about as much as possible.

34 LeRoy's use of the word "stupid" is likely a reference to how the various medicines and home remedies he was taking made him feel—groggy and perhaps a bit incoherent.

35 Dr. Spencer's Vegetable, Anti-Bilious and Anti-Dyspectic Pills was a mercury-free purgative or laxative, widely advertised in the newspapers of the day

36 Belladonna is a poisonous plant, its leaves and root used to make medicine since ancient times. Atropine is derived from Belladonna, is effective at relaxing muscle spasms.

Thursday April 3d 1862: … There is still a lurking pain in my hip which worries me at night very much.[37]

Friday April 4th 1862: … The pain in my hip has returned and I had to take a Dover's Powder last night. … I have been sick since and took a little brandy and had a poultice put on me.

Saturday Apr 5th 1862: … I was quite sick all night and not able to get up today at all. Pain in my hip very bad.

Sabbath day April 6th 1862: … I slept a great deal better last night than I have done in a good while before. I was suffering the most terrible pain when I took the Dover's Powder, and it gave me relief almost instantaneous. I took a Blue Pill last night, and am in terror of a dose of oil.[38] … Took Blue mass again.

Monday April 7th 1862: … Slept tolerable. Took Citrate of Magnesia.[39] I have eaten literally nothing since Saturday but tea and feel very weak.

Tuesday April 8th 1862: … Dr. Fitzgerald came to see me and prescribed some stuff for me to take 3 times a day. … I am up and feel tolerable. … My leg pains me just enough to keep me awake at night.

Wednesday April 9th 1862: … I commenced to take my medicine today.

Thursday April 10th 1862: …I have had a head ache and felt dull and stupid all day. I slept very bad last night.

Friday April 11th 1862: … Not much of importance occurred in the long, dull, painful day. I lay in bed all day.

Saturday April 12th 1862: … Slept bad. Had to take a small Dover's Powder. I am out of bed today. Nothing in the world seemed to agree with me. I threw up yesterday morn. I have not had a bit of appetite; I do believe I've got regular Dyspepsia [indigestion]. have stopped taking my medicine.[40]

Sunday April 13th 1862: … My leg hurts me a good deal in the night, and is pretty bad now. … My appetite is a "leetle" better today, always fluctuating.

---

37 This persistent lurking hip pain is continuing to suggest possible tuberculous involvement there.

38 Castor oil, which was used as a laxative and the bane of children for generations. LeRoy's lack of activity, together with the opium found in Dover's Powder, would have made him constipated.

39 A laxative.

40 We do not know what Dr. Fitzgerald prescribed for LeRoy, but it obviously made him so sick that he stopped taking it.

Teusday April 15th 1862: … Slept tolerably, but was annoyed by my cough. … Coughing very bad.

Wednesday April 16th 1862: … Suffered terribly with headache all night and all day today. It is aggravated by my cough which has returned as bad as in my worst days; expectorating all the time.[41] When I cough it feels as if my head would come open. I lay perfectly quiet all day but it is as bad as possible. My leg is a good deal better today. … I am not able to write hardly at all.

Thursday April 17th 1862: … Suffered with headache all night and have still got it. I took a Dover's Powder and I counted the strokes of the hour from nine till four.

Friday April 18th 1862: … I took an anodyne.[42] My head was very bad and still pains me. Cough bad. Slept very heavily. Nose bled several times.

Saturday April 19th 1862: … Pain in my head still very bad. I can not explain it at all.

Sabbath day April 20th 1862 A.D.: … Took an anodyne pill and slept until 10 oclock. My head is better today, though it ached all night. … My cough is pretty bad, and I take a gargle for it. Father rubbed my throat last night.

Monday April 21st 1862: … Slept tolerable [but my] cough, very hard.

Tuesday April 22nd 1862: … Did not sleep well. Father went to the plantation in the morn.

Wednesday April 23d 1862: … Slept well.

Thursday April 24th 1862, A.D.: … My cough is better today.

Saturday April 26th 1862: … Slept well.

Sunday April 27th 1862: … Could not rest well last night on acct of a sort of soreness of the muscles of the abdomen, which hurt me very bad when I coughed. At 1 oclock. Father got up and gave me a pill.

Thursday May 1st 1862: … My cough is annoying beyond measure. I had to take an Anodyne for it last night.

---

41 The pulmonary tuberculosis is flaring. Some writers spoke of a seasonal fluctuation in symptoms.

42 An anodyne (a common medical term before the 20th century) is a substance used to reduce pain or discomfort. Today we refer to them as analgesics or painkillers. Because so many things could be an anodyne (from a narcotic to an herb), it is impossible to know what he was taking without more information.

Friday May 2nd 1862: ... I slept very badly last night. Took an Anodyne pill. ... My cough is constant and annoys me very much. I have quit coffee + tea.

Saturday May 3d 1862: . . . Slept tolerable. No News.

Sunday May 4th 1862: ... It is 5 years ago since I first lay down. It will soon be two since I laid down this time, and I often wonder whether I am going to get well again. My back is in a great deal worse condition than it was the other time. I [wish] there were a Doctor that "could tell" me something.[43]

Tuesday May 13th 1862: ... My back hurt me last night and I had to take a pill. Cough troublesome. ... Everybody gone down town. Pain in my back too bad for me to go.

Wednesday May 14th 1862: ... I was so sore last night I took a pill and feel better today.

Thursday May 15th 1862: ... Felt very weak and sore on going to bed last night aggravated by a continual hacking cough and took an anodyne pill as I have done for 4 nights past. Slept a greater part of the morn. ... Cough very hard and dry.

Friday May 16th 1862: ... Cough very bad.

Saturday May 17th 1862: ... Went to sleep at 3.A.M. Took an anodyne. Coughed all night. Did not get up to breakfast. Father bought me some quinine pills to stop the fever I have every eve.[44]

Monday May 19th 1862: ... Spent a very bad night. Cough annoying beyond measure. Pain in my back very bad. All my nice cough medicine is gone and I can get no more.

Tuesday May 20th 1862: ... Took a Dover's Powder.

Wednesday May 21st 1862: ... Had to take a Dover's Powder to stop my cough. Had a violent coughing spell this morn. Went to sleep at 3 A.M.

---

43 Five years before this date would be May 4, 1857, seven and a half months after the injury that crushed LeRoy's leg. We suspect that the first prescription of rest was given because of suspicion of pulmonary tuberculosis when he was 9 ½ years old. Apparently he recovered enough to be able to get up and to move about with difficulty and assistance until the summer of 1860, when his physical condition deteriorated and Dr. Pancoast again prescribed the "rest cure," the two-year anniversary of which would be arriving in the coming month. People with chronic conditions such as LeRoy's yearn for a definitive answer to why they are suffering and when it will end.

44 This is the first time LeRoy mentions that he is spiking a fever "every eve." Fever in advanced consumption typically occurs in the evenings and becomes diurnal.

Thursday May 22nd 1862: ... Dr. White of Milledgeville called to see me today. He examined my back thoroughly and prescribed for my cough. He says I must take iron too. ... My cough is a little better.

Friday May 23d 1862: ... Dr. White came to see me again today, and washed my throat with a solution of caustic. [45] He recommended Porter for me. There is a man in Milledgeville who makes my cough medicine.

Saturday May 24th 1862: ... I commenced to take my new medicine today. It has no taste hardly, and I don't think I'll mind it.

Sabbath day May 25th 1862: ... My cough [indecipherable] throat is a little better for a time.

Tuesday May 27th 1862: ... I have slept well the last two or 3 nights having had scarcely any fever. My cough is better.

Wednesday May 28th 1862: ... I have had a slow headache all day.

Thursday May 29th 1862: ... Slept miserably and feel sore all over today. ... Dr. White sent over my medicine today. ... Touched my throat with "Nitrate of Silver."[46]

Saturday May 31st 1862: ... Slept well – took a dose of my new medicine and it is - - - "nasty."

Sabbath day June 1st 1862: ... Slept tolerable.

Tuesday June 3d 1862: ... My cough is Troublesome. ... I have just got over a terrible coughing spell which completed exhausted me. Dr. Fitzgerald cauterized my throat.[47]

Sabbath day June 8th 1862: ... Got a letter from Dr. White giving directions about medicines.

Monday June 9th 1862: ... Father bought 2 dozen bottles of Porter today.

Teusday June 10th 1862: ... Cough better.

Thursday June 12th 1862: ... My cough continues better.

---

45 Expectoration and swallowing of highly infectious Mycobacteria could result in tuberculous pharyngitis. Drinking or gargling caustic liquids was intended to counter the inflammation in the throat.

46 Silver nitrate is used to cauterize hyper-granulating open wounds.

47 LeRoy mentions this so casually it is hard to know what to make of it. He did not mention bleeding problems, or how his throat was cauterized, so the exact procedure is something of a mystery.

Sunday June 15th 1862: ... Had a bad coughing spell today. Went to sleep this evening and took a good nap.

Monday June 16th 1862: ... I have been annoyed by a continual hacking cough all the evening. I took some of my cough medicine, but it did'nt seem to do any good.

Teusday June 17th 1862: ... Slight pain in my hip.

Wednesday June 18th 1862: ... I coughed so bad last night that I could not sleep so I got up and got in bed with Thomas. ... I took the new medicine twice but it did no good. ... My cough is no better, and I can't do it any good. ... Took a good nap in the evening.

Friday June 20th 1862: ... Commenced to take Dr. White's medicine today. ... My cough is a little better although it troubles me some yet.

Monday June 23rd 1862: ... Have had a headache all the evening and do not feel well.

Wednesday June 25th 1862: ... I had a little fever last night and did not go to sleep till after 12. Thursday June 26th 1862: ... I was really sick this morning before I got up.

Monday June 30th 1862: ... My cough is very bad.

Friday July 4th 1862: ... I slept very badly and feel sore in all my bones this morning.

Saturday July 5th 1862: ... Have got a slight pain in my hip from my ride. ...

Friday July 11th 1862: ... We ate today the two first watermelons of the season: one was white and the other red meat. I could not enjoy mine on account of my harassing and violent cough. It is my chief trouble and wears me away.

Monday July 14th 1862: ... Since yesterday morning my cough has not annoyed me at all.

Sabbath day July 20th 1862: ... My cough, yesterday, returned and this morning my breast has a strange soreness in it and I have been coughing badly. My leg is all drawn up and I am unwell. ... Right after eating I had a bad coughing spell.

Monday July 21st 1862: ... My breast was sore enough all night and is no better today.[48]

Tuesday July 22nd 1862: ... Cough bad as ever and I can hardly eat with any comfort.

Friday July 25th 1862: ... Last night I suffered very much and could not sleep.

Wednesday August 6th 1862: ... My cough is better today more tomorrow. Leg "in statu quo."

Saturday August 9th 1862: ... I suffer very much with the heat.

Monday August 11th 1862: Hot! Hot! Hot! Hot! Hot! as fire all night and fiery again today. The Mercury [at] 8PM [was] 90°. I was very restless all night and today; my leg is so drawn up I can hardly put my foot to the floor.

Tuesday August 12th 1862: ... My leg hurts me very bad.

Wednesday August 13th 1862: ... I have a stigh [sty] upon my eye. My back pained me all night and gave me no rest hardly.

Thursday August 14th 1862: ... Spent a miserable restless night and woke more tired than when I went to bed.

Friday August 15th 1862: ... My cough worries me very much today and yesterday.

Saturday August 16th 1862: ... Ate a melon and then I coughed awfully. My cough is not improved a bit as yet. ...My leg gets no better at all.

Sunday August 17th 1862: ... Slept well last night. Took a good nap today.

Monday August 18th 1862: ... My leg is very badly drawn up and does not get any better.

Tuesday August 19th 1862: ... Slept very well. Father got me some iron pills.

Thursday August 21st 1862: ... My leg hurts me some and continues to be badly drawn up.[49] I am trying Iron Pills because I can't get any other medicine.

Saturday August 23rd 1862: ... Took some porter [beer] on going to bed and slept better than usual.

---

48 This could be muscular chest pain from chronic coughing, or pain from pulmonary tuberculosis itself, irritating the pleura of the chest cavity.

49 Paralysis and spasm of the lower extremity was the result of the vertebral collapse and impingement on the spinal cord from Pott's disease.

Wednesday August 27th 1862: ... My cough has been bothering me a good deal.

Friday August 29th 1862: ... When I first got in bed I slept very well but woke up and had an exhausting fit of coughing which kept me awake a long time.

Saturday August 30th 1862: ... I drank Porter before getting in bed but was never more restless in my life. Slept with Father too.

Sabbath day August 31st 1862: ... I have got another stigh [sty] upon my eye and I put some pain extractor on it. . . . My eye hurts me very much, and I have a headache.

Monday September 1st 1862: ... My eye hurts me very badly. Rained in the night. ... My cough worries me at times during the day. Alfred Edwards is walking on crutches. My leg is "all" drawn up.[50]

Thursday September 4th 1862: ... Slept miserable.

Friday September 5th 1862: ... I took a ride in the carriage round by the C.S. Armory and then way out by Brown's regiment. I saw them on dress parade and they looked first rate. I saw Colonel Brown + Cousin Charlie. After staying as long as I wanted to, we came home and I do not feel at all worse for my ride.

Sabbath day September 7th 1862: . . . Ate onions for dinner and am now in misery from the smell.

Friday September 12th 1862: ... My leg grows more and more crooked and I can bearly put it to the floor.[51]

Saturday September 13th 1862: ... My Dr. Pancoast is division surgeon of Old Kearney's division and the "piece" said was going to embalm his body. To see anything about him (Dr P., not Kearney) makes me want to see him more than ever.[52]

Monday September 15th 1862: ... My cough has been better for a week.

---

50 There is a tinge of frustration and even envy in LeRoy's statement. Like himself, eleven-year-old Alfred Edwards had been seriously injured. He had both hips broken in a fall from a tree on June 23, 1862; but while he was getting better and could now use crutches, LeRoy was never able to easily use crutches, and his condition was slowly but steadily deteriorating.

51 LeRoy's leg contractures have worsened because of nerve damage, and he can no longer straighten it sufficiently to touch the floor.

52 Dr. Pancoast, it will be recalled, was the Philadelphia physician LeRoy and his father visited in 1860 when LeRoy began keeping his journal. He thought highly of Pancoast, and firmly believed (indeed, hoped beyond reason) he could help him.

Teusday September 16th 1862: ... My leg is very bad and the skin and muscles are very sore indeed, so that when I stretch out the pain is bad.

Wednesday September 17th 1862: ... My leg is very bad; kept me awake nearly all night.

Thursday September 18th 1862: ... I feel sore and tired today beyond measure and slept very little after tea. Had an exhausting fit of coughing, a little worse than I ever remember to have had before.

Friday September 19th 1862: ... Slept pretty quiet after taking some Porter and cough medicine, and feel a drop better now.

Saturday September 20th 1862: ... Dr. Scherzer called to see me. Father called on him for the reason there's no one else.[53] He examined and listened as the other doctors did, and presented 2 medicines and a salve, fresh air, +c. He is foreign in his manner.

Sunday September 21st 1862: . . . Drizzled "off and on" through the day. Cough very bad at intervals. Florence is 6 years old, and 6 long years have rolled by since my leg was broken. Then began my troubles.

Monday September 22nd 1862: ... Commenced to take Dr. Scherzer's medicine No. 1 + 2 alternately, 4 times a day.

Tuesday September 23rd 1862: ... My cough is "sorter" "so so."

Friday September 26th 1862: ... Ate a "pile" of shrimps and had the night-horse [diarrhea] in consequence.

Saturday September 27th 1862: ... My cough is about the same. Have fits of it once or twice a day.

Monday September 29th 1862: ... Dr. Scherzer called; ordered my medicine to be taken every 2 hrs. ... My back hurts me today, though my cough is quiet for a wonder.

Teusday September 30th 1862: ... Pain in my back and leg very bad all night and my good leg is a little affected.[54] Took Porter on going to bed. . . . My appetite to day is so very funny. I could eat – nothing at all.

---

53 Dr. Scherzer was a local Macon homeopathic physician who trained at Hahnemann Medical College in Philadelphia. We do not know what he specifically prescribed, though LeRoy later refers to one medicine as a powder.

54 This is LeRoy's first reference to the leg that was not severely injured in the 1856 chimney collapse. Until now we did not know with certainty whether it was affected to some degree, but apparently it was not.

Wednesday October 1st 1862: … Slept miserable and feel bad in proportion today. Took some Porter on retiring which had the delightful effect of making me sick at the stomach. Coughed at intervals in the night and today.

Thursday October 2nd 1862: … I was very restless all night.

Friday October 3d 1862: … My back is better but cough only "so so."

Saturday September [October] 4th 1862: … I feel "out of sorts" and have put Sep. instead of October, and took medicine No 1 instead of No 2.[55] My cough is bad I had one hard spell yesterday and 2 today and it makes me so weak.

Sunday October 5th 1862: … Cough is very annoying.

Monday October 6th 1862: … Occupied myself with coughing instead of sleeping, and my leg is worse drawn up than ever. … Commenced to take Dr. Scherzer's powder for my cough.[56] They have no taste whatever.

Teusday October 7th 1862: … I slept very well last night. … My cough comes and goes; is better and again worse and then better again.

Friday October 10th 1862: … Dr. Scherzer called. … Last night my leg + back pained me so bad I was unable to sleep with comfort. My cough does not improve.

Saturday October 11th 1862: … Took Porter and my leg hurt me all night. In the day though no actual pain; there is a sense of uneasiness and weariness about it which is very annoying.

Sunday October 12th 1862: … My leg is if possible worse drawn up than I ever saw it. It has ached like a tooth +c; no position is easy.

Monday October 13th 1862: . . . Dr. Scherzer called + brought me a supply of Powders. … My cough isnotsoobstreperousasusual.

Tuesday October 14 1862: … My leg is better.

Wednesday October 15th 1862: … Cough and leg middling.

Saturday October 18th 1862: … Slept well. Cough miserable and I am now exhausted by a hard fit of it. It distresses me beyond measure.

Monday October 20 1862: … Coughed incessantly all the morn. … My medicine is out.

---

55 He seems to be confused, probably from his medicines and insomnia.

56 The origin and composition of this remedy remains unknown.

Teusday October 21 1862: ... Cough incessantly all night and all the morn. If my cough is not stopped it will wear me out. It depresses me beyond measure. Dr. Scherzer's medicine is a farce! My cough + leg have been awful today.

Wednesday October 22nd 1862: ... Took an anodyne pill last night. Cough not quite as bad – Leg not painful. Dr. Scherzer called +c, put 3 or 4 drops of stuff in one tumbler of water + 3 or 4 in another, and then to take a table-spoonful every hour.

Thursday October 23d 1862: ... Cough so bad had to take morphine on retiring.

Friday October 24th 1862: ... My leg pained me and my cough worried me last night and this morn my right leg, my only good leg, is slightly contracted. If it gets worse then may I truly exclaim, "I am on my last legs."[57] There are two spots one on each side of the spine on the large muscle, about as big as a silver dollar which are very tender + and pain me when I cough, from the pulling I suppose.[58] The "Hiccough" is "sufficit" to say intolerable. My only relief from the cough is in the "Syrup of Lettuce." {"Finis."}

Saturday October 25th 1862: ... My cough is miserable – wearsome – harassing – and gives me little rest night or day. It is worse when I lay on my left side.

Sunday October 26th 1862: . . . Cough a little more quiet + my rest better though I say it with fear + trembling lest it should start now.

Sunday October 27th 1862: ... Slept very well. . .. Cough comparatively quiet.

Tuesday October 28th 1862: ... Cough quiet.

Wednesday October 29th 1862: ... Cough obstreperous in the early morning then quiet all day.

Thursday October 30th 1862: ... Coughed a little in the early morn.

Sunday November 2nd 1862: . . . Had a bad spell of coughing and threw up my breakfast.

Monday November 3d 1862: ... I had a most miserable fit of coughing, sick stomach, throwing up, +c.

57 Despite all his pain and discomfort, LeRoy is still able to maintain a sense of humor.

58 "Cold" or "hot" paraspinal abscesses from spinal tuberculosis, associated with the progressive, now bilateral, neurologic symptoms in the lower extremities.

Wednesday November 5th 1862: ... Coughed all night so that what sleep I got was troubled, and after I came down had a hard fit of coughing. I always feel depressed when I cough so.]

Thursday November 6th 1862: ... My cough was distressing in the night and would not let me sleep at all.

Friday November 7th 1862: ... Took a morphine pill and my cough did not worry me quite so much. ... Dr. Scherzer called and made prescriptions.

Saturday November 8th 1862: ... My syrup of Lettuce came from Milledgeville also and it tastes altogether different from the other. I took a pill yesternight but my cough would worry me in the night. I put on my boots this morn and hardly had strength to do it.

Sunday November 9th 1862: ... I slept a while last night and then woke up + coughed a while then went to sleep again and woke up and coughed again and took some medicine. And so on alternately till morning when my Master became as quiet as a lamb. I can not venture to poke my nose out from under the cover lest I should offend him. My leg continues as crooked as ever but hardly ever pains me. I hardly dare to hope it will ever be straight again.

Monday November 11th [sic] 1862: ... Had a bad coughing spell about midnight. ... My leg is very painful to night.

11th Nov. 1862 Teusday: ... My 15th Birthday. It is 38 months since I laid down and nearly 6 long years since this disease started and today it is worse and I [am] weaker than ever before![59] ... I had to take morphine last night for my leg pained me more than it has since the time of Presbytery. ... My leg is worse drawn up than ever before. ...

Wednesday November 12th 1862: ... My cough has worried me today a great deal. I have had 3 bad spells and my new medicine has no effect. My leg aches like a tooth and I am out of sorts generally. ... I have coughed if possible more than I ever did before in one day. ... I don't have much hope, if any, that my cough will be better.

---

59 LeRoy's injury was on September 21, 1856. He indicates here that his "disease" started sometime after November 11, 1856, less than ("nearly") six years before this date. This correlates with the May 4, 1857 date suggested in a prior entry that was written in this journal on May 4, 1862. The 38 months of lying down is probably actually 28, since the instruction from Dr. Pancoast in Philadelphia on June 22, 1860. This is another clear indication the debility followed the back injury by some months. His clinical course has been one of progressive deterioration. An element of pessimism is setting in.

Thursday November 13th 1862: … Coughed a good deal. I am about in the same condition now as I was the 1st winter I was sick. That is, I can hardly get along at night without anodyne. … 9PM: coughing constantly.

Friday November 14th 1862: … Took an anodyne and my cough was quiet in the night. …My cough has been as (bad) possible all day.

Saturday November 15th 1862: … I coughed in the night and the muscles on the side of the spine very sore indeed. … I can hardly write at all for the position in which I lie makes me cough badly.

Sunday November 16th 1862: … I do not cough "much" early in the night but about midnight it starts and then there is no more rest for me until I cough up the p[h]legm. I am sadly anxious about this for fear it will (if it is not already) seriously injur[e] my lungs and thinking about this often makes me very cross + irritable as well as low spirited. I am grieved to say my cough medicine is a bust.

Monday November 17th 1862: … I took an anodyne last night + did not cough any.

Tuesday November 18th 1862: … My cough has been a little more manageable today. My right leg continues badly drawn up (I meant to say my left) but don't hurt.

Wednesday November 19th 1862: … Slept very bad on account of my cough and the room being so hot. Took a pill.

Thursday November 20th 1862: … My cough is a little quiet.

Saturday November 22nd 1862: … My cough is comparatively quiet.

Monday Nov 24th 1862: … My cough is comparatively quiet.

Thursday November 27th 1862: … Dr. Scherzer called and I am inclined to think it will be about the last.[60]

 Friday November 28th 1862:… My cough is a little worse. I slept splendidly last night. I am the Boomerang.

Saturday November 29th 1862: … Cough a little quieter.

Monday December 1st 1862: … I did not sleep well. My old cough worried me.

Tuesday Dec. 2nd 1862: … Spent a most doleful miserable night. I coughed all the morning long as well as all night long. The two spots on either side of my

---

60 LeRoy is not happy with his current doctor. He will be dismissed within the week.

spine were as sore as any thing could be. I am inclined to think that there is a matter gathered down there. It has the feeling of a very tender bruise. ...

Wednesday December 3d 1862: ... Took a pill and did not cough any in the night. My cough is in full force. Dr. White being in town, Father got him to see me. He said there was a decided tendency to abscess and prescribed Iodine to scatter the matter. He prescribed the same hyperphosphites as before. Said it was a misfortune I had allowed my leg to become drawn up by holding it in a constrained position. Father was fortunate in getting a bottle of Hyperphosphite already prepared at Zeilins [store]. He rather encouraged me to sit up. This is about the sum of what he said. ... This is official: I have dismissed Dr. Scherzer. ... Father bought me 3 gallons of Dr. Bowen's catawba wine.

Thursday December 4th 1862: ... Slept well and took ½ of a pill. Did not cough much. ... Father painted the tender places on my back with Iodine and it made 'em black and caused them to Itch.Friday December 5th 1862: ... Took ½ of a pill. My cough was quiet.

Saturday December 6th 1862: ... Took ½ of a pill. ... The Iodine made my back sting like smoke last night.

Sabbath day December 7th 1862: ... Mother bought me a bottle of "Spalding's Blue." Dr. White encouraged me try and straiten my leg but in my opinion it is hopelessly contracted. The muscle seems to have become too short. ...

Monday December 8th 1862: ... Coughed badly in the night. ... My leg is miserable. ...My cough is wearing me out.

Tuesday December 9th 1862: ... I took a ½ pill and my cough started 2 or 3 times in the night, but we checked it by drinking a little water. ... When I cough much it makes me sore. I have just coughed enough to annoy me today.

Wednesday December 10th 1862: ... Spent a bad night, notwithstanding I took a ½ of a pill 1/24 of a grain of Morphine. I coughed a great deal. I am getting more and more hopeless about this cough. I think it more closely connected with my lungs than my back. I get very down about it sometimes, and think it will never get any better. My leg is no better. I do not say this in a complaining or 'whining spirit [2 lines scratched out].

Thursday December 11th 1862: ... Took ½ of a grain of Morphia. My cough is very hard to control. ... Father found two ingredients of my medicine: Hyperphosphites of Lime + Soda. ... I have tried a little chess but find my self incomparatively dull. My cough . . . My cough wearies me, uses me up.

Friday December 12th 1862: ... Went to spend the day at Cousin Eliza's and enjoyed myself very well. . .. We had a fine dinner: Jelly, Cake, Pudding,

Bavarian Cream +c. Julia Ann went and waited on me at dinner[61] and for a wonder I did not cough any. I was glad....

Saturday Dec 13th 1862: ... I slept remarkably well did not cough + did not take a pill.

Sunday December 14th 1862: ... Father painted my back with "Iodine" and [it] itched so bad I like to run mad, and today the skin peels off and it is right raw. I put lard on it. ...My leg is drawn up as far as it can be. ...

Monday December 15th 1862: ... Slept most miserably. My back itched worse than anything I ever conceived of. It was intolerable. We tried everything to allay it. I have not coughed any in two days.

Wednesday December 17th 1862: ... My cough is not so obstreperous.

Thursday December 18th 1862: ... Cough quiet; the spots on my back are very tender indeed. ... I am the boomerang said the [incomplete].

Saturday December 20th 1862: ... I coughed and threw up my breakfast and have felt sick all day.

Sabbath day December 21st 1862: ... Coughed a good deal in the night. Had to take some Painkiller to kill a belly ache I had.

Monday December 22nd 1862: ... I slept well. I did not cough until today. I have been really sick from eating too many ribs. ... "Saw off my leg." My leg is worse than ever today. ...

Tuesday December 23d 1862: ... The spots on my back are tender beyond description. ... I rode down town for the first time in over 6 months and found the town as lively as possible in anticipation of Christmas. When I came home I was sorer than 13 boils but that didn't do it.

December 25th 1862: ... My back is evidently worse. The abscess on the left side is decided as to be plainly felt and there is a sharp pain in it when I cough. I am anxious about it as I can be. ... I have coughed a great deal and that two hard fits of it. ... I close this record with the earnest hope that ere another Christmas is gone we may have peace and prosperity! So note it to be and another earnest wish that ere that, the crisis of my disease may have passed and I may be released from the constant confinement of a horizontal position! God grant it may be so!

Friday December 26th 1862: ... I coughed all night and this morning too.

---

61 LeRoy was likely unable to sit at table with the others and so needed assistance.

Saturday December 27th 1862: ... Took a Morphine pill and feel awfully stupid today.

Sunday Dec 28th 1862: ... Cough in the night. Took Morphine.

Monday December 29th 1862: ... Slept under the influence of morphine.

Tuesday December 30th 1862: ... I got up last night and had a midnight coughing spell. Father bought me a new medicine a Syrup of HyperPhosphate, a sort of chemical food recommended by the celebrated Dr. Jackson of Philadelphia.[62] It will do to take until I can get a supply of Dr. White's medicine, as mine is nearly out.

December 25th 1863: I am no better than I was a year ago: 2 sores running constantly. [Posted as an addendum to the end of the journal.]

Volume 5
January 1, 1863 – April 30, 1864

Thursday January 1st 1863: ... I was very sick all night. I had a pain which beginning in my stomach, finally went round to my back. I took whisky, Painkiller, and Morphine and applied an iron to my side but nothing did any good and it wore off towards day. ... I have been very stupid all day from the effects of the Morphine...

Friday January 2nd 1863: ... Slept miserably. Got pain in my breast + shoulder and feel sore all over.

Saturday January 3d 1863: . . . I did not sleep but very little and feel sore all over. My medicine, the Hyph. Potassae, has come from Charleston, and Mr. Massenburg will make it when Dr. White sends the recipe.

Sunday January 4th 1863: ... Took ½ pill last night and feel a bit better today.

Monday January 5th 1863: ... Coughed in the night a great deal.

Tuesday January 6th 1863: ... Took ½ pill. ... My leg is, if possible, worse than ever.

Wednesday January 7th 1863: ... I spent a very bad night. Had two exhausting fits of coughing. I dislike the idea of taking Morphine so much, but it is the only thing that arrests the cough.

---

62 See the discussion of Dr. Jackson's Chemical Food on page 49.

Thursday January 8th 1863: ... I was compelled to take a dose of Morphine last night. My breast hurts me when I cough.

Friday January 9th 1863: ... Had a miserable coughing spell in the night.

Saturday January 10th 1863: ... My cough was so bad I took ½ pill.

Sunday January 11th 1863: ... Did not cough in the night.

Tuesday January 13th 1863: ... The tender spot on the left side of my back was very painful all night + hurt me when I coughed. This morning it feels like it would burst. ... I lay all the evening in my night gown because my back was so tender I could not stand the rubbing of my coat.

Wednesday January 14th 1863: My back hurt me so that I took Morphine. Dr. White came to see me. He tied a bandage round my back to support it and did very little else.[63] It feels very comfortable....

Thursday January 15th 1863: ... My cough has been quiet all day.

Friday January 16th 1863: Slept finely until near day when I had a slight nightsweat which made me very uncomfortable. ...

Saturday January 17th 1863: ... Slept tolerable. ... I have had nightsweats for 2 or 3 night past and they make me feel so bad.[64] I take whisky every day now. My cough is miserable at night. My leg is drawn up so I cannot put it [within] a foot of the floor.

Sunday January 18th 1863: ... Sick all night and am hardly able to write now for my cough is never ceasing. My back hurt me very bad all night. The spots on each side are as sore as possible. I feel like I would never get well. Mother and Tom put on the bandage again and it adds some to my comfort.

Monday January 19th 1863: ... I took a pill last night.

Tuesday January 20th 1863: ... I took a ½ pill and feel some better. My back feels just like it had been bruised.

Wednesday January 21st 1863: ... Took an anodyne. My cough begins as soon as I lay down at night and unless I do something to stop it, keeps me awake all night long. My back is more tender than I can express.

---

63 The carious and crumbling spine was unable to support the weight of the upper body, causing fatigue and pain in the core muscles of the body. Wraps and corsets were of some limited help.

64 Night sweats are a classic "constitutional symptom" commonly associated with advanced active tuberculosis.

Thursday January 22nd 1863: Slept tolerably. My back is like a boil. … Commenced to take my new medicine "The Syrup of the Hypophosphite of Soda, Lime + Potassa." and it is nasty and stinks. It has name enough to cure anything.[65]

Friday January 23d 1863: Clear and cool…. Slept very well. Mother had some liquid Morphine made for me. …

Saturday January 24th 1863: … I slept very well. … The spots on my back are about the same; I have a bandage on them all the time.

Sunday January 25th 1863: … Slept very well.

Monday January 26th 1863: … I slept well, as I have done for 5 nights past.

Tuesday January 27th 1863: … Slept tolerable. …

Friday January 30th 1863: Spent a most terrible night of pain, although I took Morphine. I feel very bad today. The abscess on my back is very sore. I did not get up till after breakfast. … My leg is drawn up awfully. Went on my wagon in the eve and was taken with a violent pain in my hip and suffered very much all the time till after tea.

Saturday January 31st 1863: Last night after tea I was taken with the same pain, only tenfold worse and it was terrible. I took a heavy dose of Dover's Powder and another Morphine. I cough until late in the night and every time it felt like it would kill me. My left leg did not hurt me a drop. I have lain perfectly still all day not daring to move a peg lest it start the pain again.

Sunday February 1st 1863: … I took a dose of Morphine. I did not cough till near day. I made an effort and put on my pants and was rolled into the sitting room.[66] My hip and shoulder are sore from lying on them, and I cannot lay on my other side because I cough all the time. The abscess I wish would come to a point…

Monday February 2nd 1863: Sick, Sick, Slept under Morphine. Laid very quiet all day. I wrote in here today for every day since the 28th from memory and pencil notes. I have not been able to write before at all. I don't expect to have any comfort till this abscess is lanced. Took Citrate Magnesia. It is a long ways the worst turn I ever had…

---

65 See the discussion of the newest fad in the treatment of tuberculosis in the 1860's, hypophosphites, Churchill's Specific Remedy for Consumption, pages 7-9, 48.

66 LeRoy may have had a chair or small sofa with wheels for use in the house.

Tuesday February 3d 1863: … Coughed all night. … Did not get up to breakfast. My leg is better and so is the abscess. … I was taken with a swimming in the head after tea.

Wednesday February 4th 1863: … Took Morphine. Did not cough. Dr. White called. Expressed himself satisfied with the action of the bandage + prescribed a liniment. … The swimming in my head still continues, when I sit up. I have not taken my medicine since I was taken worse. 3 oclock: Was taken sick after dinner and threw up.

Thursday February 5th 1863: … Took Morph. Grandma made me a bandage that laces up + it is a great deal better than the other.[67] My cough is pretty bad. … I have been more comfortable today than I have in some time, although I have coughed a good deal. The abscess is very tender. … Since I have had the laced bandage I have been a great deal more comfortable.

Friday February 6th 1863: … I slept very well and without an opiate. … Rubbed with Dr. White's liniment. . . .

Saturday February 7th 1863: Slept well. … My back hurts me whenever I set up. Every night nearly I have a sweat. Father got me a bottle of brandy to take for it.

Sunday February 8th 1863: Slept well in the early part of the night, but towards day the abscess pained me a good deal + this morning it is red + inflamed. … I do wish this concern would either break or go away.

Monday February 9th 1863: … Abscess exceedingly inflamed + painful beyond measure. I am strongly inclined to think that it will have to be lanced. Lay in bed all day. Had fever toward night. Coughed very hard and it hurt my back awfully. Mother + Cousin Annie went down town. Bought … Morphine pills to make me sleep. Took Morph last night.

Tuesday February 10th 1863: Slept quietly under the influence of a pill. . . My back got to be so terribly painful that Dr. Fitzgerald was sent for. He came after tea + prescribed a poultice. The pain I suffer when I cough from the jolting of the abscess is worse than I can describe and I dread to lance it. It is red just like a boil and as tender too.

Wednesday February 11th 1863: Took 1/12 grain Morph and then 1/12 in fluid form. I coughed incessantly last night till ten oclock and every time it looked like I could stand it no longer. Had a poultice of flaxseed put on which feels very

---

67 A homemade corset to provide back support.

nasty. ... Towards night had an exhausting fit of coughing. ... [I am] sick in bed. I do not relish any thing but beef tea [broth] + ice cream.

Thursday February 12th 1863: ... Took 1/8 grain Morph which had the effect of keeping me wide awake till near day though perfectly quiet and unconcerned whether I slept or not. Took [Citrate] Magnesia before breakfast. I do not have any ease and will not till this thing is opened. The Dr. came at dinner to lance it but I was not ready and so he came again at 4½ and all that time I had the pleasure of anticipating it. It hurt me a good deal and when I strained as if to cough the matter gushed out and it ran a great deal.[68] After it quit running, Dr. Fitzgerald put a tent in to keep it open and then a poultice.[69]

Friday February 13th 1863: ... Took 1/8 grain Morph. The poultice was taken off at dinner time and soon this morn, and it had ran a great deal both times. Laid on my left side all day so as to let it run. My cough has not worried me.

Saturday February 14th 1863: ... Took ½ pill. Took off the poultice and put on a greasy cloth. ... I sweat heavily every night and have until yesterday had fever in the evening. Had beef tea.

Sunday February 15th 1863: . . . I would have slept very well but for the heavy + exhausting night sweat which took away my comfort. Got into bed with Father. Took brandy. The Dr. came to see me last night. As proof conclusive that this concern would have bursted, another hole beside the one the lancet made has broken. It ran "right smart" this morn. ... My back ran a great deal when it was dressed at night. I take brandy 3 times per diem.

Monday February 16th 1863: Slept well, that is for me. ... The relief I experience since the abscess was lanced is inexpressible.

Tuesday February 17th 1863: ... Slept tolerable. ... My cough is quiet. My back has not hurt me any.

Wednesday February 18 1863: ... Slept well.

Thursday February 19 1863: ... Abscess itched a great deal in the night.

---

68 It sounds as though the abscess pointed and drained spontaneously, although LeRoy subsequently talks about relief obtained since the abscess was lanced.

69 A tente was a conical mass of linen filaments folded in half and twisted, giving it a spiral shape. It was used to dilate a fistulous channel that was too small to allow the free escape of pus. For a fuller treatment of the use of such dressings in the management of wounds during the Civil War, see D.A. Rasbach, "Civil War Dressings—Lint," in C. E. Loperfido, *Death, Disease, and Life at War* (Savas Beatie, 2018), 126-131.

Friday February 20th 1863: … Woke up about two oclock with a bad pain in my stomach and nought would relive it. It must certainly have some connection with my back.

Saturday February 21st 1863: … Took ½ pill. I am suffering very much with weakness in my back. I can hardly sit up at all.

Sunday Feb 22nd 1863: . . . My back is better. I am not so weak as I was yesterday + day before.

Monday February 23d 1863: … Slept good.

Wednesday February 25th 1863: … Grandma dressed my back. … My cough is quiet.

Macon Thursday Feb 26th 1863: … Slept well and enjoyed my breakfast very much.

Friday February 27th 1863: … My back does not give me any pain or trouble, and is a decided improvement on the cough.

March 1st 1863: … Woke up in the night with a bad pain in my back and side. Suffered a great deal and laid in bed till noon. It is a strange pain. . ..

Monday March 2nd 1863: … Slept well. Mother and Grandma went out shopping.Tuesday March 3d 1863: … Slept well. Father sat up with Colonel Huguenin. …Wednesday March 4th 1863: … Took ½ pill. I felt so sore + weak. Did not get up till about ten AM.

Thursday March 5th 1863: … Back running [draining] very freely.

Friday March 6th 1863: . . . I spent a very restless night and feel very weak. … Went to bed feeling sore + tired and my hips both aching me.

Saturday March 7th 1863: Did not sleep well at all. …

Sunday March 8th 1863: … Felt so bad and my legs ached me so that I took a pill. I did not get up till 10½. … My back runs a great deal. … Went out on my wagon in the P.M. and rode around the garden.

Monday March 9th 1863: … Took ½ pill.

Tuesday March 10th 1863: … Took ½ pill. Both hips ached all night + whenever I move they pain me. My back is as weak as anything can be and I can't sit up without pain. The abscess runs a great deal + I feel weaker every day. Dr. Fitzgerald called.

Wednesday March 11th 1863: Sick. … I slept but little. Took 1/12 grain Morph. But the pain and soreness in my joints was so bad I could not rest. … I got 2 glasses [mirrors] + looked at my back. ... Suffered a great deal during the eve.

Thursday March 12th 1863: ... Slept tolerable. ... My leg is better. Took 1/12 grain Morphia.

Friday March 13th 1863: ... I slept pretty well and my leg did not hurt me a bit till I got up. It is my right leg and my only dependence.

Saturday March 14th 1863: ... Took a pill. My leg ached me all night. I coughed too, a horrid little hacking cough, and that kept me awake.

Sunday March 15th 1863: ... Slept – none Took 1/12 grain Morph. My leg is no better. Slept all the morn. ... My back ran a great deal today.

Monday March 16th 1863: ... Took 1/12 grain Morphine. I slept heavily till 11 oclock. I started taking "The Syrup of the Iodine of Iron" the other day, but I don't like it much.[70] ... My hips both ache me from lying on them. ... "My back runs hugely."

Wednesday March 17th 1863: ... Took Morphine. Literal I have no rest except when I am asleep, for my hips are so sore that I cannot lay on them hardly at all. I feel more discouraged, less hopeful, about getting well than I ever did before. I am weaker and more helpless than I ever was. My hip, when it is not actually paining me, has a weary feeling which makes me want to move. I sleep very little at night. Mother has made 2 little pillows to put under my back.

Friday March 20th 1863: ... Slept well. No news.

Saturday March 21st 1863: ... I did not go to sleep till very late last night. ... I am very thankful to say I feel a "great" deal stronger and am able to set up and eat and write. I hope I am thankful for it.

Sunday March 22nd 1863: ... I have had a dull headache all day and am not as well as I was yesterday. .... My appetite is miserably puny.

Monday March 23d 1863: ... Slept well.

Tuesday March 24th 1863: ... I did not sleep any till near day.

Wednesday March 25th 1863: ... Slept tolerably.

Thursday March 26th 1863: ... I am taking Iodide of Iron pills. ... I rode down town [in my wagon] but it hurt my back.

---

70 Iodide of Iron (see discussion, page 11), was used as a medication and dietary supplement since the early 19th Century. The medicine (which would soon change to pills for LeRoy) had side effects including headaches, allergic reactions, and depression.

Friday March 27th 1863: ... My back ran a great deal of bloody-looking matter last night and is very sore now.

Saturday March 28th 1863: ... I slept well. My back is not as sore as it was. ...

Monday March 30th 1863: ... I am more comfortable than usual. I am hopeless about my leg and try to be content if I am without pain.

Tuesday March 31st 1863: ... My back ran a great deal at the last dressing.

Wednesday March 32nd 1863: ... Slept tolerable. ... My [good] right leg hurts me and it is slightly contracted. I don't feel well a bit.

Thursday April 2nd 1863: ... I feel a little better today. ...

Friday April 3d 1863: ... My back runs as much as ever.

Sunday April 5th 1863: ... My back has grown very sore since dinner. The abscess ran very little the last two times it was dressed.

Monday April 6th 1863: ... Lay in bed all day feeling very miserable from the consciousness that another abscess has started to form just opposite the other one. It is as sore as possible. I am glad my cough is not bad. ...

Tuesday April 7th 1863: ... Took a Morphine pill. Minnie on a pallet in the back parlor. The Dr. called to see me. Confirmed our opinion as to an abscess. Prescribed Poulticing; I had one on yesterday. Abscess runs very little. ... I do dread more than I can tell another abscess.

Wednesday April 8th 1863: ... In bed. Abscess ran very little.

Friday April 10th 1863: ... My abscess does not run and the other one does not increase. I am afraid I'll have a long and painful siege before it opens. It is very tender.

Saturday April 11th 1863: Took 1/12 grain Morphine. I feel very bad. Abscess just runs enough to keep the new one back but not enough to carry it off. I slept nearly all the eve.

Sunday April 12th 1863: Spent a miserable night of pain and feel tired to day. I wish this abscess would form. ... I can't wear my pants at all. My appetite is miserable.

Monday April 13th 1863: ... I feel a little better. The abscess ran a little more and the sore place on the other side don't increase in size but is still tender. ...

Tuesday April 14th 1863: ... I am troubled with a bad cold and snuffle continually. ...My cold is worse and I feel pretty bad I will take a small Dover's Powder tonight.

Wednesday April 15th 1863: ... Took a Dover last night and am in bed today.

Thursday April 16th 1863: ... I am well of my cold.

Sabbath day April 19th 1863: ... My back run a great deal today. The tender spot continues about the same. . ..

Monday April 20th 1863: ... My back pains me today. The coming abscess is very prominent and will have to be lanced.

Tuesday April 21st 1863: ... My back has hurt me all day. The abscess on the right side has risen again. ... The abscess runs perhaps more than it ever did. ... Toward night the pain grew very bad and no position was easy to me.

Wednesday April 22nd 1863: ... Took Morphine and my back was so very painful; we applied a poultice. I slept nearly all day. ...

Thursday April 23d 1863: ... Took Morphine. Put a nice flaxseed poultice on my back and the sore ran a great deal. The rising has decreased in size. I am anxious for it to form and be done with it. I have not been out of bed; my back + legs ache so.

Friday April 24th 1863: ... Slept well. Lay in bed all day. . . I have had fever for a week past every evening. The Abscess runs immensely! My appetite very poor.

Saturday April 25th 1863: ... My back ran a great deal in the morn and then ran so tremendously it had to be dressed in the middle of the day. ...

Monday April 27th 1863: ... I rode out on my wagon into the vegetable garden the 1st time in a month...

Tuesday April 28th 1863: ... The rising on my back was very sore all night. Sometimes it looks like it would open + then it subsides again. ... My back runs so much that we can't keep it from getting on my clothes. The rising hurts like a boil.

Wednesday April 29th 1863: ... My back runs hugely. ... There is no comfort in lying down.

Sabbath May 3d 1863: . . . The rising [abscess] is very prominent + hurts a good deal. ...Monday May 4th 1863: ...I took Morphine. Abscess was poulticed all night and again today. Dr. Fitzgerald lanced it at 4½ oclock and it hurt a great deal because it was not as ready to open as the other was, and the cut had to be made deeper.[71] I lay in bed all day dreading it and I could not eat till it was done. I

---

71 There was no local anesthetic in LeRoy's time. An abscess that is pointing and very close to the surface is easy to drain with minimal discomfort, but a deeper abscess would have been quite uncomfortable to lance if chloroform or ether was not administered.

do hope it may benefit me. I took a glass of wine previous to having it opened. …
Took a pill at about 7 oclock.

Teusday May 5th 1863: … Suffered a great deal till after midnight when
Mother + Father got up, removed the poultice + dressed my back. After that I was
a great deal more comfortable. … Father fixes my back.

Wednesday May 5th 1863: … Slept well. Back [abscess] no. 1 ran lots; No 2
none, so we put a poultice on that till dinnertime. It does not run any and it looks
like it would heal up. … It is a great bother to dress my back and takes 2 to do it.

Thursday May 6th 1863: … My back has healed up again. It itched so last night
that I could hardly stand it.

Friday May 7th 1863: … Back running very little. …

Saturday May 9th 1863: … Slept well. … Back runs but little. Went in my
wagon and stayed nearly all the eve.

Sunday May 10th 1863: … Put on white breeches. My abscess on the right ran a
little.…

Wednesday May 13th 1863: … New abscess ran a little. The [draining] matter
is very thin indeed.

May 16th Saturday 1863: … My crutches came last night. I am very, very weak
and can-not take many steps. … I feel weak + bad today.

Monday May 18th 1863: … I am quite unwell. Took paregoric last night.[72] …
My Back has hurt me all day and itchd very bad.

Tuesday May 19th 1863: … The itching of my back at times is intolerable. …

Wednesday May 20th 1863: … Took Morphia. The itching of my back was
beyond endurance.

Thursday May 21st 1863: … New abscess runs the most now.

Tuesday June 2nd 1863: … I rode out on my wagon and it made me feel so sore
that I did not sleep hardly at all.

Wednesday June 3d 1863: . . . I have no appetite for several days and have not
[felt] well at all. . . . I get along well enough with my back but my leg will never
be straight…

Monday June 8th 1863: ·… My back runs a great deal now. …

---

72 Paregoric, which contained opium, was found in many households in 19th century. It
was widely used to combat diarrhea and as a cough medicine.

Tuesday June 8th 1863: ... My back runs hugely.

Thursday June 11th 1863: . . . I did not sleep well. I had such a binding pain across the chest and I think it comes from overexertion. My leg distresses me greatly and worse than all, folks say it's my own fault, I can straiten it if I would try.[73] Well ~~ . . . Friedapplesaregoodandsoispig.

Friday June 12th 1863: ... The pain in my breast is better. ...

Sunday June 14th 1863: ... Went to bed feeling dizzy and my head aches now.

Monday June 15th 1863: ... Woke up with headache. Took a blue pill.

June 16th 1863: ... I did not sleep well at all. I had a pain in my head + right hip but feel very well today. ...

June 17th Wednesday 1863: ... My back ran a great deal of dark bloody looking matter last night.

Monday June 22nd 1863: ... My right leg pains me a little.

Thursday June 25th 1863: ... Did not sleep well. ...

Monday June 29th 1863: ... My back has not run much the last week.

Tuesday June 30th 1863: ... Thomas had to dress my back. The "new un" [abscess] has not run a drop in a day and night. I hope it'll heal up.

Saturday July 4th 1863: ... 3 years ago I laid down and it has not done me any good. My left leg is worse drawn up than ever. Father brought me some pills: "Dr. Blanchard's Iodide of Iron." I commenced to take them. Do not feel very well today.

Friday July 10th 1863: ... My back has been weak as a baby's for two or 3 days and my leg hurts me a little.

Saturday July 11th 1863: ... Slept poorly. My leg and side hurt me very bad.

Sunday July 12th 1863: ...I am hopeless about my leg; it is drawn so bad. Father is too.

Monday July 13th 1863: ... I wish I had something to do, now the days are so long + I get so tired.

Tuesday July 14th 1863: ... I am sore + tired today. ...

---

73 LeRoy is understandably indignant about this kind of statement by people who have not been through his experience of constant pain and a mix of treatments that usually do not work.

Thursday July 16th 1863: ... Did not sleep well. A little old Dog got into the yard and squealed + hollered the whole night at intervals and dogs run cows in the alley, and then my leg hurt me very bad at first. ... My back run tremendously yesterday.

Friday July 17th 1863: ... I did not sleep but very little last night on acct of my leg +c.

Saturday July 18th 1863: ... My leg pains me more than usual today and I feel very sore all over.

Sunday July 19th 1863: ... I did not get up to breakfast this morning; my back felt so bad. My back runs profusely. I cannot keep it off my clothes.

Monday July 20th 1863: ... My back runs hugely.

Monday July 27th 1863: ... Rode over to Mrs. Huguenin's and looked at the puppies +c, and am now as tired as I can be from the jolting. ...

Tuesday July 28th 1863: ... Back runs but little. ...

August 1st 1863 Saturday: ...Slept miserably. My old abscess hurt me very bad. . . Have felt bad all day.

August Sabbath 2nd: . . . Slept badly, did not get up till after breakfast. ... My leg is hopeless. Father tries to straiten it, rubs it, tries to cheer me, but It will never be straight.

Tuesday August 4th 1863: ... Slept very badly and did not get up 'till after breakfast. My back felt so bad. ...

Wednesday August 5th 1863: ... Slept badly had some fever, I think, and feel sore and tired today. We ate a watermelon in the morn and one in the even + both times when I tried to eat, I coughed so I had to quit. . .

Thursday the 6th August 1863: ... Feel better today. Slept better too. ...

Sunday August 9th 1863: ... I suffer a good deal with heat. ...

Tuesday August 11th 1863 1863: ... Suffered much last night with heat.

Monday August 24th 1863: ... My back never gives me any trouble now and I never notice it in my diary. It is dressed regularly as "pigs tracks" every morn + eve. Hereafter every Sunday I will tell how it has been through the week.

Wednesday August 26th 1863: ... My Back has been very comfortable all day.

Friday August 28th 1863: ... Slept most miserably on acct [of] a pain in my breast caused by riding too much on my wagon, and I do not feel much better today. ... My leg hurts me very bad.Saturday August 29th 1863: ... I took an anodyne as I was sick and in pain. … My leg hurts me some today, my good leg, too.

Thursday Sep 3d 1863: … Slept miserably. …

Friday September 4th 1863: … Slept better. …

Sunday September 13th 1863: … I have got a very bad cold. My back felt sore and tired. …

Wednesday September 16th 1863: … My back [abscess] has now run out all over me.

Sunday Sep 20th 1863: … My back runs a great deal and annoys me by running on my clothes. For a day or so it has been very sore indeed.

Monday Sep 21st 1863: … My back feels very weak + bad. …

Monday October 5th 1863: … My good leg aches like a tooth.

Thursday October 15th 1863: … My back hurts me and feels very weak indeed. … Did not sleep well at all last night.

Friday October 16th 1863: … Passed a restless night. …

Saturday October 17th 1863: … I have been very unwell for two or 3 days, no appetite.

Monday October 26th 1863: … My back runs immensely.

Tuesday October 27th 1863: … Made me a new bandage [for my back].

Wednesday October 28th 1863: … Nothing worth noting occurs in the dull routine of my daily life.

Thursday November 5th 1863: … My back has run but little for a day or so.

Tuesday November 10th 1863: … My back is very sore. …

Wednesday November 11th 1863: … This is my 16th birthday.[74]

Sunday Nov 15th 1863: … I have sat up more in the last week than I have in 3 years before and I hope no bad effects will result from it. …

---

74 This is the first birthday that passed without LeRoy noting any fanfare or receiving any gifts.

Monday 16th Nov 1863: ... We all went to Cousin Jimmie Snider's and weighed. I weighed 63 pounds;[75] Wilson 71. Took my measure for some crutches. ...

Tuesday November 17th 1863: ... My back hurt me last night. Slept well though.

Thursday November 19th 1863: ... Passed a bad night: had an awful headache and pain in my hip and considerable fever.

Friday November 20th 1863: ... I have been quite unwell for a day or two.

Sunday November 29th 1863: ... My back has run but very little for a day or so and I have coughed a little at night. How soon the cough would return would the issue to stop!

Saturday December 12th 1863: ... My Back has been running a great deal in the past day or two.

December 14th 1863: ... I took a cold last night + am bad off for a dose of "Peach [brandy]."

Wednesday December 16th: ... My cold is no better.

Thursday Dec 17th 1863: ... Did not rest well at all. ...

Friday December 18th 1863: . . . I do not sleep well that is I do not go to sleep 'till late.

Monday Dec 21st 1863: ... The pain in my leg was so bad that I had to take a Dover's Powder.

Tuesday December 22nd 1863: ... I suffered a good deal last night, did not sleep well + could not get up to breakfast. The pain is much worse at night.

Wednesday December 23d 1863: ... My leg was very bad + I took a little Morphia. ... My back is very weak. ...

Volume 6
January 1, 1864 – January 8, 1865

Sunday January 3d 1864: ... My Back is not running much at all. . ..

---

75 Evidence of profound emaciation—a sixteen-year-old male weighing 63 pounds. This is unrelenting consumption!

Monday January 4th 1864: ... I am afraid I am going to have pain in my leg again but I hope with a night's rest I will be better.

Tuesday January 5th 1864: ... I am better of that pain in my leg today. "I am the boomerang" said the Wild Man!

January 7th: ... Every body but me has gone to Cousin Eliza's to a family dining, given to cousin George and his bride. ... My back is very weak and hurts me when I sit up.

Thursday Jan 28th 1864: ... Spent a bad night: had pain in my hip. ... I have a pain in my hip, which gives me some trouble.

Friday January 29th 1864: ... Took an anodyne pill last night, and did not go to sleep till two oclock. I have suffered a great deal today: the pain is just like Rheumatism, and worse than all is in my strait leg.

Saturday Jan 30th 1864: The pain in my hip has been very bad all day. I took a Dover's Powder last night and got along pretty well. ...

Sunday Jan 31st 1864: ... My leg just hurt me bad enough to keep me awake last night, and still aches a little. ...

Monday February 1st 1864: ... Took a Dover's Powder. My leg hurt me very bad. It is much worse at night.

Tuesday February 2nd 1864: ... My leg is a good deal better today.

Sunday February 7th 1864: ... It seems to me that as I grow older, the weary, monotonous life I lead seems more burdensome. If I just had some regular employment, I could get along better: sleeping + eating embrace all my time....

Monday February 15th 1864: ... My back feels weak and bad enough.

Tuesday February 16th 1864: ... I had the Rheumatism in my leg last night.

Wednesday February 17th 1864: ... My throat is miserably sore and I feel badly. This is the first bad sore-throat I ever had. Rubbed with liniment.

Thursday February 18th 1864: ... My throat continues very sore.

Friday February 19th 1864: ... Throat a little better.

Sunday February 21st 1864: ... My throat is well and my cold has settled in my head.

Sunday February 28th 1864: ... I have had a cold for two weeks and it is hard for me to get rid of it. . ..

Monday Feb 29th 1864: ... My cold hangs on to me yet. I have had it three weeks. I cough a good deal at night.

Tuesday March 1st 1864: ... Took a Dover's Powder for my cold, but it is no better.

Wednesday March 2nd 1864: ... My cold and cough continue to annoy me, and do not get any better.

Thursday March 3d 1864: ... My cold has settled down into a cough and it annoys me a great deal at night.

Friday March 4th 1864: ... My cough worried me a good deal in the night.

Tuesday March 8th 1864: ... I have had a dull headache all day and if it does not improve tomorrow I must take some medicine for it. My cold is no better.

Wednesday March 9th 1864: ... My head still aching. ... Mother and I have both got coughs and we cough all day + night. ... Took Blue Mass.

Thursday March 10th 1864: ... My head is better. Did not sleep well.

Sunday March 13th 1864: ... My cold is well: it hung on a long time though. ...

Wednesday March 23d 1864: ... My Back on a very very low average, has run 1000 teaspoonsfull since Feb. 11th 1863![76]

Wednesday March 30th 1864: ... I am not well at all: have a bad pain in my breast + back.

Tuesday April 12th 1864: ... I coughed very badly all yesterday and took a Dover's Powder last night. I feel most dull and stupid. Layed in the dark, in the Parlor + tried to sleep off the effects of the medicine. I am taking the measles; cough incessantly, took Brown Mixture for it.[77] ...

Wednesday April 13th 1864: ... Last night took a Dover's Powder for my cough. About 3 oclock in the night was taken with toothache + I have suffered tortures today.

Thur. Apr 14th 64: Took a Morphine pill and though I did not sleep well my tooth got easy. ... I broke out thick with measles this morn and have been very sick all day. Dr. came to see me but said I was doing first rate. Coughing a good deal.

Friday Apr. 15th 1864: ... I have been better today and the eruption is not so thick.

---

76 LeRoy has estimated that he has lost 1000 teaspoons of fluid since February 11, 1863.

77 Another opiate mixture with extract of licorice root, tartar emetic, and spirit of ethyl nitrite glycerol, meant to work as an expectorant.

Saturday April 16th 1864: Coughed a good deal in the night + took Brown Mixture for it. … Eruption paler on me + cough better.

Sunday Apr 17th 1864: … Took a hot Milk Punch last night at bedtime. …I am a good deal better and the eruption is disappearing.

Monday April 18th 1864: Minnie and I convalescing. … Nothing tastes natural to me and I have not a particle of appetite.

Wednesday Apr. 20th 1864: … I slept tolerably and, with the exception of a cold in the head, am well as usual. … My cough troubles me a good deal yet and I am not troubled with appetite.

Thursday April 21st 1864: … Last night at supper was taken sick, threw up and coughed badly. Went to bed + took a dose of Paragoric.[78] About 12 oclock in the night took another dose and I have slept 'till 11 AM + do not feel able to get out of bed. …

Friday April 22nd 1864: … Slept tolerably and got out of bed again today. … Have coughed a great deal today.

Saturday April 23rd 1864: Slept miserably: kept awake by cough. Took Paragoric at 2 oclock. … Went on my wagon for first time. …

Sunday April 24th 1864: … My cough is better.

Monday April 25th 1864: … Slept badly: but feel a constant disposition to sleep in the day.Wednesday April 27th 1864: … Taken with a sort of pain in my back at 4 oclock.

Thursday April 28th 1864: … Suffered with pain in my back till midnight; then took a Morphine pill and got easy about 1 AM. Felt so unwell that I did not get out of bed at all till about 5 oclock.

Friday April 29th 1864: … Feel better today. No news. …

Sunday May 15th 1864: … Took 20 drops [of] laudanum to check Diarrhea. … My leg ached all night.

Monday May 23d 1864: … My leg + back pained me all night. One joint of my spine, right between the abscesses is very sore and you can see the matter, as it

---

78 Another tincture of opium, this time mixed with benzoic acid and anise oil, used to control diarrhea.

runs from that joint to the abscess, which proves that, as long as there is any disease there, the sores cannot heal.[79]

Thursday 26th May 1864: ... I Was restless and excited and could not sleep last night 'till towards morning.

Wednesday June 1st 1864: ... Could not sleep much on account of pain in my leg. Have suffered a good deal today. Took some medicine for my bowels.

Monday June 6th 1864: ... Am taking 2 iron pills per day. Dr. Hall sent only 6 for me to try. ...

Friday June 17th 1864: ... I passed a most miserable night + feel weary and depressed. ...

Saturday June 18th 1864: ... I woke up with a pain in my breast and I have hardly been able to sit up at all.

Sunday June 19th 1864: ... My breast is well. I did not sleep well.

Tuesday June 21st 1864: ... I spent a bad night with pain in my leg + back and O! how glad I was when morning dawned!

Tuesday July 5th 1864: ... This day I enter on the fifth year of my confinement to my couch: 5 long and weary years! I am much worse off now than then.[80]

Tuesday July 12th 1864: ... My leg pained me much this evening and I fear I will spend a bad night.

Wednesday July 13th 1864: ... Spent a wakeful night of pain. . ..

Sunday July 17th 1864: ... I have caught a cold + cough and snuffle continually.

Monday July 18th 1864: ... Took Paragoric last night and slept all this morn. I have caught cold and have a very bad cough. ...

Saturday July 30th 1864: ... I passed a very bad night: my leg + back pained me so much that I could only toss and roll all night.

---

79 LeRoy is very perceptive. The carious destruction of the spine by the tubercle bacillus is the source of his problem. He is probably referring to the sharp angle of the gibbus deformity as the "joint of the spine." As long as infection and decayed matter persist there, the soft tissue ulcers and abscesses will not heal.

80 Four years of confinement completed—apparently beginning five days after he returned to Macon on June 30, 1860 with instructions from Dr. Pancoast; now entering the fifth year of the "rest cure" and, sadly, only deterioration to show for it.

Sunday July 31, 1864: … I took a Dover's Powder and I slept better than the night before. … I have been free from pain today. The "dover" cured me.

Friday August 5th 1864: … I have had a pain in my right shoulder and side and it hurts me when I breathe. …

Thursday August 11th 1864: … Have sat up too much today and I reckon on a bad night. If the left hand abscess ceases running one day, it gives me a pain in my back + draws up my leg worse.

Friday August 12th 1864: … Passed a restless uneasy night.

Tuesday August 16th 1864: … I have got a boil on my side and it pains me a good deal.

Thursday August 18th 1864: … My Boil on the side not well yet.

Friday August 19th 1864: … I have not mentioned my back in a long time. For over a year past it has been dressed twice a day regularly after breakfast and at bedtime. The left hand abscess runs at least 4 times as much as the right hand one. They do not give me much trouble and I have come to think that they will stay open as long as I live. …

Monday August 22nd 1864: … I was taken with a pain in my hip after tea last night and I have been very restless all day.

Tuesday Aug. 23rd 1864: … Was in so much pain that I took a Dover's Powder and consequently passed a quiet night. Did not get up till 11½ A.M. I am quite easy now. …

Wednesday August 24th 1864: … My leg is well again.

Tuesday August 30th 1864: … Had pain in my back yesterday evening and I am not entirely free from it yet.

Saturday Sept 3d 1864: … I went to bed at 11 oclock with it determined that the enemy had overwhelmed us and contrary to my expectations went to sleep directly.

Thursday September 15th 1864: … I have been really sick all the evening.

Friday September 16th 1864: … I took a dose of Paregoric before going to bed last evening and feel better.

Wednesday November 30th 1864: … Had a bad headache all the P.M.

Thursday December 1st 1864: … Had the headache all night, but am well this morning. …

Tuesday December 6th 1864: … I am sick today with pain in my back and soreness of the old abscess. … I could not read and it diverted my mind. …

Wednesday December 7th 1864: ... Suffered all day with pain in the left abscess and I would not put on my clothes at all. I could not move without pain. Had a starch poultice on it so as to make it discharge. I never was so bad off with it since they were made.

Thursday December 8th 1864: ... Went to bed very early last night but could not sleep and about 11 Oclock, Mother got up and gave me 20 drops of laudanum, after which I rested better. I have never saw my back run so. When the dressings are off and I strain it runs in a stream. Had a poultice on all P.M. and when it was taken off it ran hugely. ...

Friday December 9th 1864: ... I am much better this morning. The running of my back has relieved me.

Sunday December 25th 1864: . . . My back has not discharged freely in the past week and so I have suffered with pain in it all day.

Monday December 26th 1864: ...I slept pretty well last night and I am well today.

1865

January 2nd 1865: ... Did not sleep well on account of a lurking pain in my hip, which has now grown to a steady ache. Worse than all it is in my right leg. ....

Tuesday January 3d 1865: ... I suffered much last night and all today. I have had a constant aching in my hip which is very annoying and hard to bear. It has drawn up my good leg too. ...

Wednesday January 4th 1865: ... Took twenty drops of laudanum and did not in consequence get to sleep till after midnight. My leg numb and painful when it is moved. My appetite is gone. I ate 3 eggs for my breakfast and a partridge which Father bought down town for my dinner. When I press on a certain spot near the right abscess I can feel a sharp pain shoot down into my hip. ...

Thursday January 5th 1865: ... I have laid in bed and on my couch all day. I slept badly: took 7 drops of laudanum. ... Toward night my throat had grown sore and I feel really sick. This is the second spell of pain I have had in my good leg. My back runs profusely.

Friday January 6th 1865: . . . Spent a miserable sleepless night but I am thankful to say I feel a little better today and hope this spell is over. ...

Saturday January 7th 1865: . . . Slept pretty well, but there is a slight pain in the hip yet. . . . I became so hoarse that I could not speak even in a common tone. Came home rather uneasy, but it got better toward night.

Volume 7
January 1, 1865 – June 8, 1865

Tuesday January 3d 1865: . . . Suffering very much with pain in my right hip.

Wednesday January 4th: . . . Took 20 drops of laudanum. Did not sleep any and have suffered very much during the day. . . .

January 5th 1865: Laid in bed until 12 noon. Father . . . Throat slightly sore.

January 6th 1865: Did not sleep hardly any, but still am better. . . .

Sunday Jan. 8th 1865: Clear and cold. Had an eggnog last night the first of our Christmas. Read Advice to Young Communicants by Dr. Jas. W. Alexander of New York City.

Monday, January 9th, 1865: . . . Lurking pain in my hip.

Tuesday, January 10th 1865: . . . Did not rest well on account of my leg. . . .

Saturday, January 14th, 1865: . . . My leg is not well yet and every time I go out in the cold, it aches. . . .

Sunday, January 15th, 1865: . . . My back is running profusely and still my legs ache every night. . . .

Monday, January 23d, 1865: . . . My throat is sore a little. . . .

Tuesday, January 24th, 1865: . . . My throat is so sore I can hardly swallow. . . .

Wednesday January 25th, 1865: . . . Gargled with sage tea last night, but my throat is very sore and somewhat swelled. . . . My throat becoming ulcerated, we sent for Dr. Hall, who prescribed, Chlo. Potash [Potassium chloride] gargle.[81]

Thursday, January 26th, 1865: . . . Coughed a good deal in the night, and my throat quite sore. Dr. called 5 P.M.; pronounced it better and ordered the gargle to be continued. Pain in my back and chest.

Friday, January 27th, 1865: . . . Took a Dover's Powder last night and my throat is well.

---

81 Tuberculous pharyngitis.

Saturday, January 28th, 1865: ... I am much better this morning, but the cold is hard upon me.

Monday, January 30th, 1865: ... I have been sick with a pain in my back and heart all day. Tuesday, January 31st, 1865: ... My back ran immensely, and I feel much relieved.

Saturday, February 4th, 1865: ... I am confined to the house.

Tuesday, February 7th, 1865: ... Have had a slight pain in my hip all day: it makes me very restless.

Wednesday, February 8th, 1865: ... Slept well, notwithstanding the aching in my leg. ... My leg aching all day.

Saturday, February 11th, 1865: ... I have taken a bad snuffling cold, and feeling droopy, did not get up to the matutinal [early morning] meal. ...

Sunday, February 12th, 1865: ... My cold, better.

Thursday, March 16th, 1865: ... My daily occupation, doing nothing, is becoming more irksome to me every day. I do long for health + active employment.

Tuesday April 4th, 1865: ... I have taken slight cold.

Monday, April 17th, 1865: ... Have been suffering with Diarrhea for some days.[82] Took paregoric last night and slept nearly all the morning.

Tuesday, April 18th, 1865: ... I have been very drooping today. Dr. Hall came to see me last night + prescribed camphor + paregoric which relieved my trouble [diarrhea]. I have nausea + no appetite still.

Wednesday, April 19th, 1865: ... Lay on the sofa nearly all day + suffered no little with pain in my back. A day of unceasing pain.

Thursday, April 20th, 1865: ... I was in much pain when I went to bed last night; took a Dover's Powder and feel relieved from pain.

Friday, April 21st, 1865: ... I slept upstairs, and I slept very well notwithstanding the yanks were passing by all night. [83] ...

---

82 This is the first reference LeRoy makes to his health in some time. In fact, he was quite sick, and not referencing just how ill he was on a regular basis.

83 Robert E. Lee surrendered at Appomattox on April 9, 1865. LeRoy will become increasingly depressed as his physical condition continues to deteriorate, and as signs of the subjugation of the South become more apparent.

Thursday, April 27th, 1865: . . . Suffering with pain in my right leg – a never ceasing ache. ...

Friday, April 28th, 1865: ... I was very sick all night threw up and kept awake nearly all night by pain in my right leg and back. ...

Saturday, April 29th, 1865: Recorded as a day spent in dozing on account of Dover's Powder taken last night. In the evening suffered very much with intense pain in my right leg. Was sick and threw up my supper.

Sunday, April 30th, 1865: ... Dr. Hall called to see me this morning and examined my back + the abscesses. He is afraid to trouble them but is going to make me some tonic pills and see if he cannot relieve the indigestion + Dyspepsia from which I constantly suffer. I feel very low spirited myself + want to take something.

Monday, May 1st, 1865: ... I passed a miserable night and today my good leg is drawn up as bad as the left. It is not aching much either.

Tuesday, May 2nd, 1865: ... Took a Dover's Powder and passed an easy night but my leg pains me all the time and is badly drawn up. Dr. Hall brought me some iron pills. I never had as tedious a spell before. ...

Wednesday, May 3d, 1865: ... Took Paregoric last night and today have suffered tortures with my leg. ... I am perfectly helpless – both legs being drawn up badly. I have no appetite and if I eat it disagrees with me.[84]

Thursday, May 4th, 1865: Took a Dover's Powder but my leg is no better. . . I am very low-spirited now, I am so completely helpless with both legs contracted and one of them almost paralyzed from pain.[85]

Friday, May 5th, 1865: ... Slept miserably + feel sore and bad leg still aching.

Saturday, May 6th, 1865: ... Took a Dover's Powder last night and woke up feeling a little better; this P.M. I have suffered a good deal.

Sunday, May 7th, 1865: ... Had to take Paregoric last night + I had not much rest from pain during the latter part of the night. I long for ease and freedom from pain.

---

84 LeRoy is now routinely throwing up most or all of what he ingests. He likely has gastrointestinal tuberculosis.

85 In nearly constant pain, with paralysis of both legs, no appetite, with vomiting and diarrhea, a sore throat, his back draining rivers of pus, unable to sleep, dozing from drugs in the daytime—who would not be low-spirited in such miserable circumstances?

Monday, May 8th, 1865: ... Although I took a Dover's Powder, I rested but little and feel weak and sore. O! how much I suffer! No position in which I lie is easy and the days are long and painful + the nights weary. ...

Tuesday, May 9th, 1865: ... Took a Dover's Powder and rested very sweetly and feel a little better. ...

Wednesday, May 10th, 1865: ... Slept under [effects of] a "Dover," enjoyed my breakfast and am free from pain almost.

Thursday, May 11th, 1865: Spent the day in bed. Had an attack similar to Cholera morbus.[86] Vomited freely. Took some paregoric and today have suffered from Diarrhea. I haven't a particle of Appetite.

Friday, May 12th, 1865: ... I feel about the same today. Suffered all day with nausea and I can't touch anything to eat. Minnie and Clare deGraffenreid have taken the 1st Honor at College and Miss Flora Smith the 2nd. This was announced Wednesday but my brain is so muddled with Opium I forgot to record it. . ..

Sunday, May 14th, 1865: Slept so badly and felt so weak + sick I did not get up. Dr. Hall prescribed for me and sent me some elegant brandy to take every 4 hrs. I have never been so weak and . . . low-spirited.[87] ...

Monday, May 15th, 1865: ... Father sent some silver and got me some steak[88] which I relished eating + threw up soon after. My stomach is so weak it cannot digest anything. Dr. H[all] called. ... I am so so weak I can hardly write.

Tuesday, May 16th, 1865: ... Slept well though I am still sick and my bowels troubling me. ... I have eat nothing today but beef tea and a few raspberries and have no appetite.

Wednesday, May 17th, 1865: ... Dr. Hall came and prescribed calomel + opium. He thinks it is my liver which is disordered. Ate beef tea for breakfast + dinner. ... Dr. Hall called + prescribed a mixture for my trouble which I hope will cure me.

Thursday, May 18th, 1865: ... Am a little better.

Saturday, May 20th, 1865: Dr. Hall thinks best that I should remain in bed today and so here I am. I enjoyed very much a piece of mackeral sent to me by the

---

86 Acute gastroenteritis marked by cramps, diarrhea, and vomiting.

87 Severe depression.

88 The Greshams are now having to barter for food, as they do not have specie (coin) to use.

above doctor for my breakfast. Father bought two quarts of cherries which as they were forbidden fruit troubled me the more sorely. ...

Sunday, May 21st, 1865: ... Eat ½ broiled chicken for breakfast and the same for dinner ...

Monday, May 22nd, 1865: ... My bowels still trouble me and it does not seem to matter what I eat. I am taking Bismuth every three hrs.[89] I am in bed in the wing today.

Tuesday, May 23d, 1865: Clear and beautiful. Slept well, enjoyed my breakfast – a broiled chicken and feel better today. Have just dressed and come down into Mother's room. ... Dr. Hall pronounces me so much better today that I can eat raspberries in a week. I am to continue the Bismuth 3 times a day. I keep a lovely June Apple to smell which is delicious torture. ...

Wednesday, May 24th, 1865: ... Feel a great deal better and have a good appetite.

Friday, May 26th, 1865: ... Ate too much pig and am sick today. ... Dr. Hall called. He did nothing but caution me against imprudences in eating. ...

Saturday, May 27th, 1865: ... I feel better again this morn and hope I'll get well. My appetite is ravenous.

Sunday, May 28th, 1865: ... I am quite unwell today + feel very despondent. Dr. Hall came to see me and says the whole thing is from eating that pig.

Monday, May 29th, 1865: ... After every meal I suffer pain no matter how little I eat. My back runs a great deal.

The remainder of the entries are in Mary Gresham's hand. It reads exactly as if LeRoy was writing it, so there is little doubt he was dictating to his mother.

Tuesday May 30th 1865: ... Very unwell to-day ...

Wednesday May 31st 1865: Still in bed. Dr. Hall sees me daily. ...

Thursday June 1st 1865: ... No better to-day myself – Father improving.

Friday June 2d 1865: I am worse this morning than I was yesterday – the Doctor says that my case has assumed the form of Dysentery which he said does not dread so much as the Diarrhea I was having before.

Saturday June 3d 1865: No material change in my condition since yesterday....

---

89 An antidiarrheal, Bismuth is found in Pepto-Bismol and Kaopectate, two modern drugs that treat the same problem.

Sabbath June 4 1865: I have the same report to make to day of my health – no better. . . .

Monday June 5th 1865: . . . The Doctor comes to see me now twice daily and will continue to do so until I am better. My appetite is Vocative – wanting.[90]

Tuesday June 6th 1865: Thomas went to Market to get some beef to make tea for me which I did not I am sorry to say relish very much. Dr. Hall has prescribed a preparation of Creosote for me to take which he says is one of the best remedies known to the profession.[91] I am continually under the influence of opium which I am taking every three hours in larger quantities than I ever did before.

Thursday June 8th 1865: I have slept pretty well for the last two nights under the influence of a quarter grain of Morphia. ... I eat very little and even this nauseates me. My back runs very little now and I only dress once in two days.

Friday June 9th 1865: I am perhaps. . . .. [dying][92]

LeRoy Wiley Gresham died on June 18, 1865, precisely five years after his hopeful arrival in Philadelphia to consult with Dr. Pancoast. His father, John Jones Gresham, noted his death in the journal with these words:

(LeRoy Wiley Gresham, author of this diary, died in Macon, Ga. June 18th 1865)

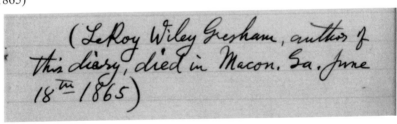

90 The fact that the doctor is now coming twice a day is a good indication of just how sick LeRoy was, although he was still not aware he was dying, and no one informed him otherwise.

91 Creosote was used to treat skin wounds and as an antiseptic. Guaiacol, a natural organic compound derived from raw creosote, was used in Europe as early as the 1830s as a treatment for tuberculosis (consumption). Its cough suppressant properties likely convinced the doctors it was doing something useful, but the remedy fell out of favor by the turn of the century. An expectorant, today known as guaifenesin, was made from creosote.

92 Nearly five years after his expectant departure for Philadelphia in search of a miraculous cure, the harsh reality sets in for LeRoy. His poor parents have been tortured with this knowledge for much longer. He has only eleven days more to live.

Bibliography

Altonen, B. Dr. *Churchill's Cure for Consumption, History and Controversy.* https://brianaltonenmph.com/6-history-of-medicine-and-pharmacy/pacific-northwest-medicine-ca-1820-ca-present/john-kennedy-bristow-1814-1883/research-papers/dr-ch urchhills-cure-for-consumption-history-and-controversy/ (accessed March 11, 2018).

A Practical Chemist, Member of Several Scientific Societies, etc., The Cyclopaedia *of Practical Receipts in all the Useful and Domestic Arts, being a Compendious Book of Reference for the Manufacturer, Tradesman, and Amateur.* London: John Churchill, 1841.

Bennett, D. "Hypophosphites in the Treatment of Phthisis." Edited by D and Blake, J Wooster. *Pacific Medical and Surgical Journal,* 4 (1861), Selections, 14.

Boardman, Thomas. A Dictionary of the Veterinary Art: Containing All the Modern Improvements . . . London: George Kearsley, 1805.

Brown, C. A. *Treatise on Scrophulous Diseases, Shewing the Good Effects of Factitious Airs: Illustrated with Cases and Observations.* London: M. Allen, 1798.

Churchill, J. F. *Consumption and Tuberculosis: Their Proximate Cause and Specific Treatment by the Hypophosphites upon the Principles of Stoechiological Medicine.* London: Longmans, Greene, and Co., 1875.

Churchill, J.F. "De la cause immedidate et du traitment specifique de la phthisie pulmonair et des maladies tuberculeuses." Paris, 1858.

Cleaveland, C. H., ed. "Churchill's Hypophosphites in Phthisis." *Journal of Rational Medicine,* 1, no. 7 (July 1860): 220.

Cooper, S. *The First Lines of the Practice of Surgery: Being an Elementary Work for Students, and a Concise Book of Reference for Practitioners.* London: Justin Hinds, 1815.

"Creosote not a specific." *Journal of the American Medical Association,* October 1898: 1062.

Culbreth, D. M. R. *Manual of Materia Medica and Pharmacology.* Philadelphia, New York, 1896.

Dutcher, A. P. *Pulmonary Tuberculosis: It's Pathology, Nature, Symptoms, Diagnosis, Prognosis, Causes, Hygiene and Medical Treatment.* Philadelphia: J. B. Lippincott & Co., 1875.

Earle, J. *The Chirurgical Works of Percivall Pott, F.R.S, Surgeon to St.Bartholomew's Hospital, a New Edition, with His Last Corrections, to which are added a Short Account of the Life of the Author . . . and Occasional Notes and Observations.* 3 vols. London: Wood and Innes, 1808.

Eberle, John, and Ducachet, H.W. *The American Medical Recorder*, Vol. 5. (Philadelphia), 1822, "On Caustic Issues," 216-224.

Firth, J. "History of Tuberculosis, Part 1 - Phthisis, consumption and the White Plague." *Journal of Military and Veterans' Health*, 22, no. 2 (June 2014): 29-35.

Fishberg, M. *Pulmonary Tuberculosis.* Philadelphia and New York: Lea & Febiger, 1919.

Garg, R. K. "Spinal Tuberculosis: A review." *J Spinal Cord Med*, 34, no. 5 (2011): 440-454.

Kelynack, T. N. "Relation of alcoholism to tuberculosis." *Transactions of the British Congress on Tuberculosis for the Prevention of Consumption*, July 1901: 336.

Kiecolt-Glaser, J. K., Glaser, R. "Depression and immune function: Central Pathways to Morbidity and Mortality." *Journal of Psychosomatic Research*, 53 (2002): 873-876.

Köhler, F. E. *Köhler's Medizinal-Pflanzen in naturgetreuen Abbildungen mit kurz erläuterndem Texte.* Gera-Untermhaus, 1887.

Lloyd, J. U. "New Remedies: Compound Syrup of the Hypophosphites and Compound Syrup of the Phosphates." edited by H. W. Felter. *The Eclectic Medical Journal*, 76, no. 10 (1916): 512-513.

Moore, J. "The use of corsetry to Treat Pott's Disease of the Spine From 19th Century Wolverhampton, England." *International Journal of Paleopathology*, 14 (Sept. 2016): 74-80.

Peltier, L. F. *Orthopedics: A History and Iconography.* Norman Publishing, 1993.

Pott, Percivall. *The Chirurgical Works of Percivall Pott, F. R. S., and Surgeon to St. Bartholomew's Hospital.* 3 vols. London: T. Lowndes [et. al.], 1783.

Rasbach, Dennis A. "Civil War Dressings—Lint." in *Death, Disease, and Life at War: The Civil War Letters of Surgeon James D. Benton, 111th and 98th New York Infantry Regiments, 1862-1865*, by Christopher E. Loperfido. California: Savas Beatie, 2018.

Reiche, E. M., Nunes, S.O., and Morimoto, H.K. "Stress, Depression, the Immune System and Cancer." *Lancet Oncol.* 10 (Oct 2004), 617-625.

Rhodehamel, E. J., Pierson, MD, and Leifer, A.M. "Hypophosphite: A Review." *Journal of Food Protection* (International Association of Milk, Food and Environmental Sanitarians), 53, no. 6 (June 1990): 513-518.

Rogers, P. K. *Observations on the Employment of Caustic Issues in the treatment of various diseases*. Vol. 5, in *The American Medical Recorder*, by Eberle, J. and Ducachet, H. W., 216-224. Philadelphia, 1822.

Sathyamoorthy, P. "Extension of Paravertebral Abscess in Tuberculosis of the Thoracic Spine: Report of Two Cases." *Medical Journal of Malaysia*, 45, no. 4 (1990): 329-334.

Tuli, S. M. "Historical Aspects of Pott's Disease (Spinal Tuberculosis) Management." *European Spine Journal*, 22 (Suppl. 4) (Jun 2013): 529-538.

"Value of Iodide of Iron." *American Journal of Medical Sciences: Quarterly Summary of the Improvements and Discoveries in the Medical Sciences*, LXXII (October 1858): 516-517.

Wilsey, A. M. *Half in Love with Easeful Death: Tuberculosis in Literature*. *Humanities Capstone Projects*. Pacific University, 2012.

Index

Read LeRoy's full diary, meet his family, and relive the lives of the Greshams in...

The War Outside My Window
The Civil War Diary of LeRoy Wiley Gresham,
1860-1865

Edited and annotated by
Janet E. Croon

Maps, illustrations, photos, footnotes, pub. preface, *dramatis personae*, biblio., Index. 480 pages. Cloth, d.j. $34.95

Where fine books are sold, or directly from the publisher: www.savasbeatie.com

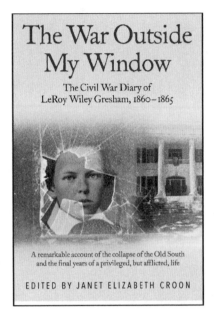

The War Outside My Window

The Civil War Diary of
LeRoy Wiley Gresham, 1860–1865

A remarkable account of the collapse of the Old South
and the final years of a privileged, but afflicted, life

EDITED BY JANET ELIZABETH CROON

About the Author

Dennis A. Rasbach, MD, is a graduate of the Johns Hopkins University School of Medicine, and a busy practicing surgeon.

He is the unlikely author of *Joshua Lawrence Chamberlain and the Petersburg Campaign: His Supposed Charge from Fort Hell, his Near-Mortal Wound, and a Civil War Myth Reconsidered* (2016), a critically acclaimed micro-history of the Civil War experience at Petersburg on June 18, 1864. While investigating the movements of his great-great-grandfather's regiment (the 21st Pennsylvania Cavalry), his focus suddenly and unexpectedly changed to Joshua Chamberlain and his famous charge when glaring contradictions emerged as the popular narrative of that event was compared with the historical record. Those inconsistencies prompted an intense search for clarification and resolution which, with help from a network of new Civil War friends, grew into his book.

Dennis is a member of the Civil War Round Table of Southwest Michigan. The father of two sons, he resides with his lovely wife Ellen in St. Joseph, Michigan. Coincidentally, his birthday is June 18, the same day of the Petersburg charge he wrote about in his first book, and the same day young LeRoy Gresham died.